Humanitarians

for Justice, Nonviolence, and Peace

Journey of an Unexpected Sculptor

Meera Censor

Sculpture photography by Colby Stephens

ISBN-13: 978-0-615-50127-7

Introduction

We live in a time that calls for "change"—change in how we care for the environment, school systems, politics, war zones, and much more. Countless organizations and people are working diligently for this, yet some people seem to forget just what the call to "change" means. Change can take a great deal of time and commitment. It can also be a single moment of realization, the decision to act in ways that enhance your life or the lives of others. Change starts from the heart; it calls for personal, as well as global, compassionate decisiveness.

> "The ultimate measure of a man is not where he stands in moments of comfort and convenience, but where he stands at times of challenge and controversy. The true neighbor will risk position, his prestige and even his life for the welfare of others. In dangerous valleys and hazardous pathways he will lift some bruised and beaten brother to a higher and more noble life."
>
> *Martin Luther King, Jr.*

The sculptures I created are of humanitarians who saw the need for change and dedicated themselves to making those changes in a nonviolent manner, sometimes at great risk—and with the understanding that change takes vigilance, a dedicated life effort. I hope that the stories of their lives give insight and inspiration for the possibility of choosing compassion over anger, integrity over greed, and courage over fear. Some of these people you have heard of; some could be new to you. All led or are leading lives dedicated to human justice through nonviolent action.

These people demonstrate the heart of nonviolent alternatives: Love. They understand that, even when there is pain, it helps everyone to look at both sides of the story and strive to see what is possible to alleviate the pain at the root of the circumstance. By choosing empathy over judgment, compassion instead of aggression—difficult conflicts then became opportunities for new ways to resolve conflict. They understood the need to change the injustice at hand, often in creative ways, reaching out to uplift others. Their lives have given me great inspiration, often at times in my life when it seemed like things were falling apart. I picked up one of their books and—in reading what they had faced and overcame using heart centered action—I said to myself, "Puts things into perspective, doesn't it Meera? Let your adversity be an opportunity."

Perhaps you too, are struggling with something. I hope reading these stories of service will give you a new perspective. I sense that, when we choose to read these stories and make compassionate choices for ourselves, we honor lives dedicated to human justice. I believe that they all understood Gandhi who said, "An eye for an eye leaves everyone blind."

Life is an interesting and often unexpected journey. When we choose to move from our heart's passion, whatever that may be, hardships turn into amazing opportunities, and a new life's work can bring gifts to others as well as to ourselves.

My decision to create these sculptures unfolded in an unusual way. When I started this project, I had no art background and was completely ignorant of the time, cost, and of course the amazing experiences that would be the result; had I been a trained artist, I may have thought twice about taking on a self-funded project like this. It took seven years to complete twenty-one pieces. Nonetheless, it has given me great joy, the opportunity to donate some of these sculptures to various organizations, fund-raising events, and place them in public places as reminders of lives dedicated to humanitarian service in challenging conditions.

We see sculptures in many public places. I always wonder about the artists and just what it took for the artist to place them there. If you are curious, like me, then I hope you enjoy reading a bit about my adventure in creating this series of sculptures. But, much more important, I hope you might be inspired to learn more about these noteworthy individuals and perhaps contribute to their causes. I am hoping that you also will be inspired to use your gifts and time in pursuit of your own creative path towards a more peaceful world. That's my dream. What you start might not make logical sense, but if your heart is calling, and your mind is challenging you, try listening to your heart. Now, if you are already doing that, I want to thank you and remind you of the importance of your efforts.

You'll see as you read along that I am enamored with people who make a difference, and I keep a collection of quotes that resonate with my values and goals. So here is a quote by David Gershon in *Social Change 2.0, A Blueprint for Reinventing Our World*, which speaks to my journey and perhaps yours as well: "If your dream is compelling enough it draws forth your passion and this keeps you motivated to stay with it even when the odds are against you. And if you stay with something long enough eventually you wring out the truths needed to bring it to fruition." That most certainly was my experience, and that of whom those I have written about in these pages. So, here in this book, I am sharing a bit of my love of humanitarians and my journey as an "unexpected sculptor."

Meera Censor

The Sculpture Series

Remembering Humanitarians

"There are moments in our lives, there are moments in a day, when we seem to see beyond the usual. Such are the moments of our greatest happiness. Such are the moments of our greatest wisdom. If one could but recall his vision by some sort of sign. It was in this hope that the arts were invented. Sign-posts on the way to what may be. Sign-posts toward greater knowledge." *Robert Henri*

I never imagined when I created my portrait of Gandhi, that this would start a huge life change that was very challenging, yet also wonderful, exciting, and definitely an unexpected journey. As a young mother with five children I never had the opportunity to study art or do much in the way of art expression. I was 26 years old before I sculpted for the first time. I had decided to take a night school pottery class, thinking I would make plates and cups for my family and get a night out for myself. Turns out, much to my surprise, I didn't enjoy the potter's wheel at all. However, in the back of the classroom, there was a woman creating a portrait sculpture. I was fascinated. I asked the teacher if I could do that instead. He agreed to let me try. So I brought in photographs of my father and started. My first attempt looked just like him. It seemed to be effortless, and the feeling of the clay in my hands was soothing, enchanting, and a bit mysterious.

It was 26 years before I had the opportunity to sculpt again. In 1997 a dear friend of mine, Chelsea McGraw, a professional muralist, asked if I had ever done any art. I told her about my first sculpture, which had long since broken in a houseful of kids. Fortunately, I did have a photograph of it and I showed Chelsea, who said, "Meera, you must sculpt again." Two weeks later, on my birthday, Chelsea surprised me with a gift of sculpting tools and clay.

I pondered who I would like to sculpt. I had always admired Mahatma Gandhi, so I decided my second sculpture would be of him. When I was finished, friends suggested that I cast it in bronze, so I took foundry classes and learned the bronze process. Several years went by, and I longed to do another sculpture, but I hesitated because of the cost of casting. Then, one day my local library asked me to put the Gandhi portrait on display for three days. After the three days, they asked if they could keep it for three more weeks because every book about Gandhi in the library was checked out. I now had a great reason to continue despite the expense. I had a voice and, by sculpting, I could share my interest in these lives. The passion for doing this series of humanitarian sculptures was born; the journey began, I became "an unexpected sculptor."

Holding clay in my hands and shaping it into a likeness is magical for me. Creating sculptures of humanitarians was a way I could share my passion for these inspiring people and their journeys from adversity to lifetime commitments towards social change. Many lived frequently dangerous lives, but were filled with a deep love of humanity and a willingness to sacrifice much for their causes. As I mentioned, I had little idea beforehand of the complexity and scope of this project. Nor could I have known the incredible experiences this project would bring. Sculpting definitely became a passion that took over my life, brought me to new places, and introduced me to many wonderful people.

At that time in my life I, like many people, had and still do have concerns about the amount of violence in the media. As a mother and grandmother I was particularly worried. I had an idea that by creating sculptures of people who were dedicated to nonviolent social change, I could perhaps counteract some of the effects of violent media with powerful stories about a different perspective, alternatives to violence. My plan was to take those sculptures into schools and share with children stories of these dedicated humanitarians. To date, I have had the opportunity to speak to hundreds of schoolchildren. That experience is always truly rewarding.

People often ask me how I choose my subjects. There are literally hundreds of thousands of people, most not well-known, who would fit into this series. There is no shortage of visionaries—just a shortage of visibility. However, I have limited myself to twenty-one sculptures, with hopefully another two in the future, to keep the collection at a manageable size. It was important to me to include different ethnic and cultural backgrounds, so I chose people from a variety of cultures and countries. Perhaps my viewers would see someone familiar to their ancestry and be inspired by their accomplishments.

The order of creation of these sculptures seemed to have a life of its own. The method is falling in love with the person and their story, having great respect and admiration for their commitment and sacrifice, and taking the time to read all of the books I can to find out about their journey and their personality. When I finally choose a look or an expression to capture, it represents a mood or a moment that is in some way compatible with their life and work.

Mahatma Gandhi 1869-1948

In my early life I experienced intense discrimination, a pain that many of us experience at some time in our lives. In reading Gandhi's book, *My Experiments with Truth,* I read of his experience of discrimination, internal struggles and remarkable triumphs. I was deeply touched. He was an inspiration for me, for many of the people in this series, and continues as an inspiration for many others in the world today.

Pondering the life of Gandhi, I remembered how meditation and contemplation were most important to him, so sculpting him with eyes closed in meditation symbolizes his deep spirituality and commitment to internal guidance.

A timely book I also recommend is *A Man to Match his Mountains: Badshah Khan Nonviolent Soldier of Islam* by Eknath Easwaran. This book is timely because, as American forces persist in Afghanistan, I believe that it is important for us to understand the Afghan people and their culture. This book says a great deal to educate us in that respect. Abdul Ghaffar Khan (1890–1988) and Gandhi formed a deep friendship based on their dedication to nonviolence. A devout Muslim, Khan's story is one to ponder, as well.

"Nonviolence is the greatest force at the disposal of mankind. It is mightier than the mightiest weapon of destruction devised by the ingenuity of man."

Mahatma Gandhi

Badshah Khan chose nonviolence out of his dedication to the deepest aspect his faith and out of true respect for Gandhi. He chose to stand for nonviolence at a time in Afghan history when violence was common; however, many chose to follow his lead. I wanted to create a sculpture of Badshah Khan but was unable to due to limited finances. Since I could not, I wanted to mention him in this book in hopes that I could inspire you to read about his life and work. You will learn of the treasured independence of the Afghan people, their culture, and the commitment to nonviolence that this man fully embraced.

Please visit **www.gandhiinstitute.org** as there is much to learn there.

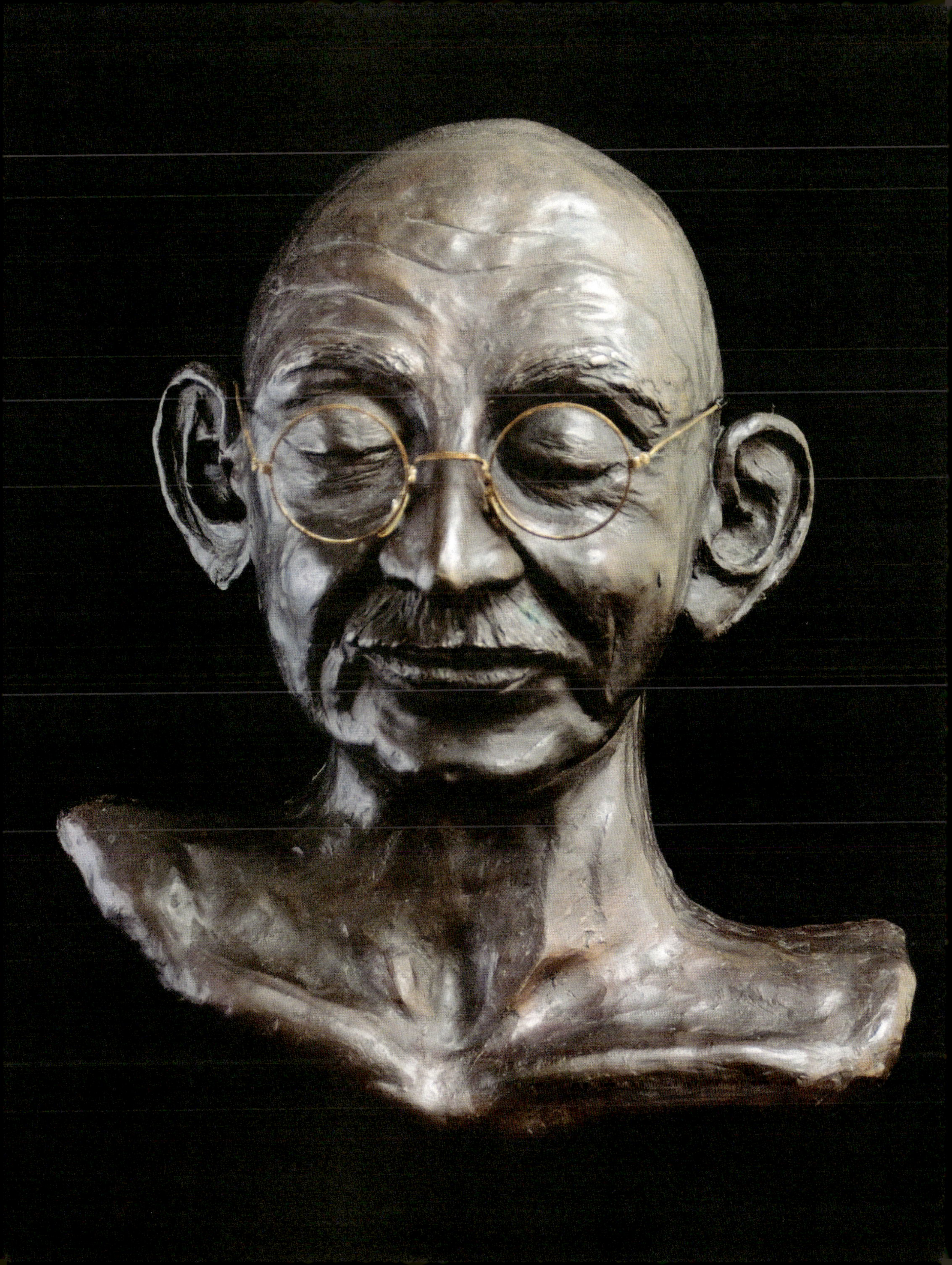

Kasturabai Gandhi 1869-1944

Kasturabai Gandhi followed her husband to prison, shared his three-week fasts, and fully shared the burden of his responsibilities. All this she did while raising their children. Her spiritual strength encouraged and inspired Gandhi. She was dedicated to his life's work and mission. Gandhi said, "I learned the lesson of nonviolence from my wife."

"I learned the lesson of nonviolence from my wife. Her determined resistance to my will on the one hand, and her quiet submission in the suffering my stupidity involved on the other hand, ultimately made me ashamed of myself and cured me of my stupidity."

Mahatma Gandhi

Kasturabai was imprisoned for protesting British rule. She died while still in prison, after sixty-two years of marriage to Mahatma Gandhi. Gandhi said after her death, "She was an indivisible part of me; no woman could move me as she could."

I hope that, when you see the sculptures, you will consider reading not only about Mahatma Gandhi but also about the life of Kasturabai. I recommend *The Forgotten Woman* by Arun and Sunanda Gandhi to get a clear insight on her honorable character. It is hard to find any direct quotes of Kasturabai, so I have chosen some by her husband.

"Woman is the companion of man, gifted with equal mental capacities. She has the right to participate in the minutest details in the activities of man, and she has an equal right of freedom and liberty with him."

Mahatma Gandhi

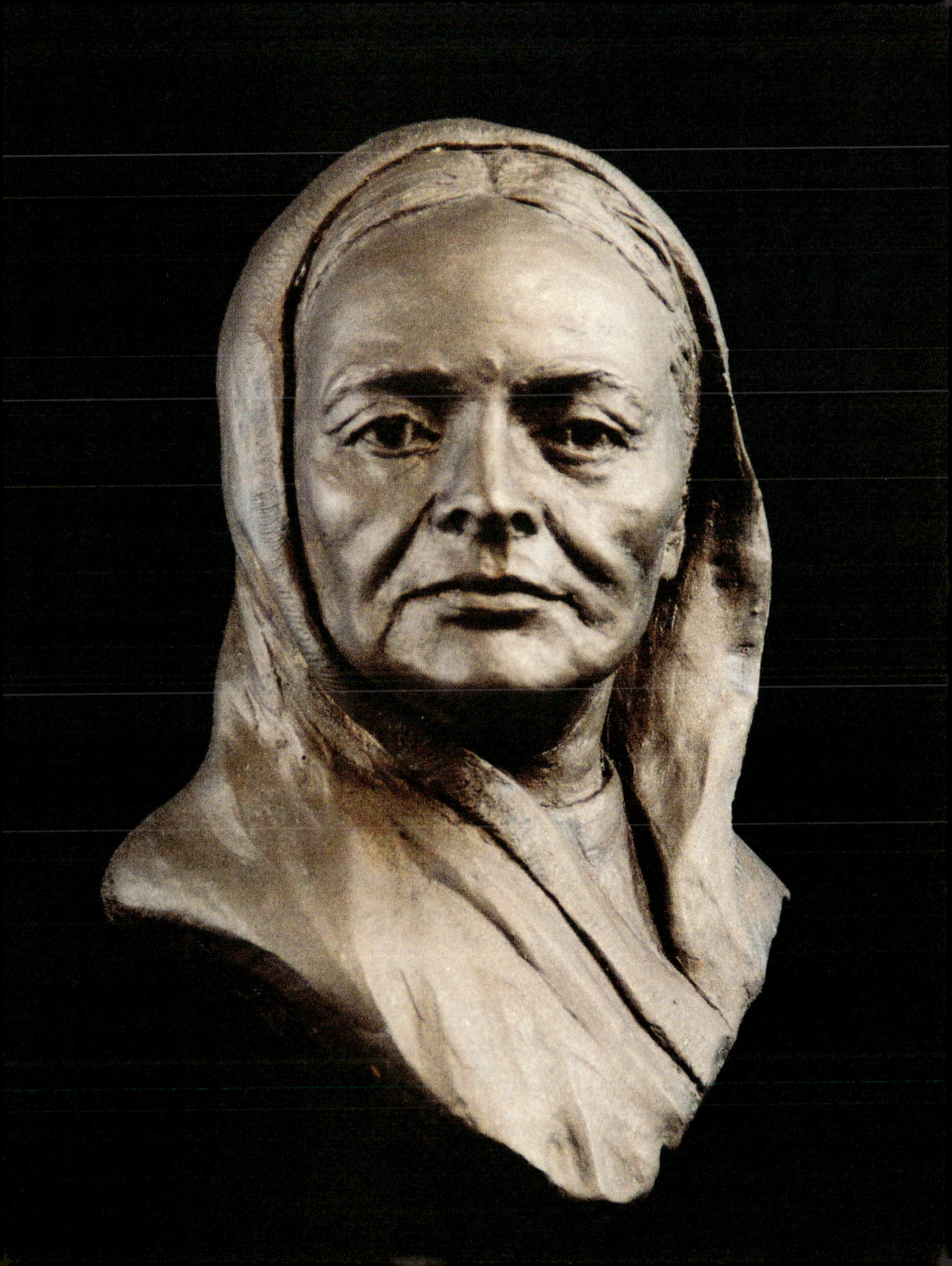

Martin Luther King, Jr. 1929-1968

I read the story of how Martin Luther King, Jr. and his wife made a trip to India to study Gandhi's methods for their movement for equality. Therefore, King was my next choice. I have been truly inspired by his actions, speeches, books, and definitely his courage. When I read any speech of his, much emotion arises in my heart. Such a gifted orator and writer. How grateful we should all be that this man chose to give his life to the cause of equality, inspiring so many, and opening hearts and minds.

"Injustice anywhere is a threat to justice everywhere."

Martin Luther King, Jr.

When I started sculpting, I didn't know that Dr. King is a particularly difficult likeness to create. One of my mentors, master sculptor Christopher Pardell, later shared that insight with me. Working from photos or videos of Dr. King presented a challenge as his weight and age changed over the years. His face is very beautiful, but his look changes dramatically at different angles. If you look at various sculptures of King, you will find many different interpretations—I did my best at the time, but nothing matches the beauty of King's energy.

Christopher was a great asset to me. From him, I learned how to make molds, a necessary skill for a sculptor. He even let me use his studio for my work. His expert guidance and generosity was an offering of his kindness.

Read more at **www.TheKingCenter.org**.

"Everybody can become great because everyone can serve."

Martin Luther King, Jr.

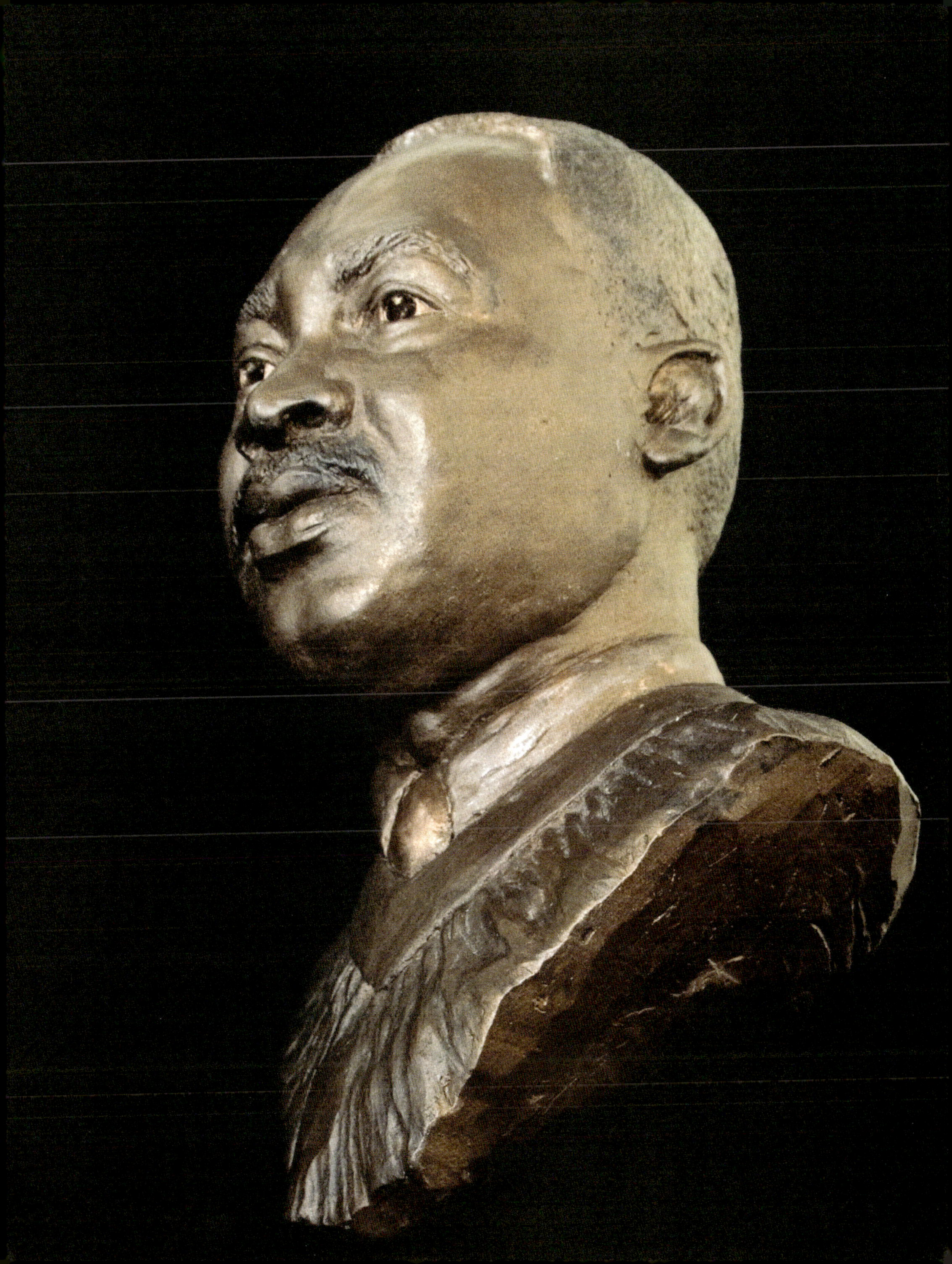

Mother Teresa 1910-1997

Next, I created a sculpture of Mother Teresa, an Albanian Catholic nun known for her work in India with the poorest of the poor. I thought about the important impact of her life and knew she belonged in this series for many reasons. She upheld nonviolence by honoring the humanity in all people, no matter that their religious beliefs differed from her own. Serving humanity from the heart, so naturally and with such passion, is a quality shared by all my subjects; in her, it was a well-known trait. She spoke about the importance of compassion, service and great love, and she lived what she spoke.

"Love has no meaning if it isn't shared. Love has to be put into action. You have to love without expectation, to do something for love itself, not for what you may receive. If you expect something in return, then it isn't love, because true love is loving without conditions and expectations."

Mother Teresa

A copy of the Mother Teresa sculpture is in a hospital in Los Angeles. I donated it to a group of Carmelite nuns I happened to meet one day, walking down the street. I gave them the sculpture, and they decided to place it in the hospital where it could inspire people to look at their difficulties through Mother Teresa's eyes.

Visit **www.motherteresa.org**.

"People are often unreasonable, irrational, and self-centered. Forgive them anyway. If you are kind, people may accuse you of selfish, ulterior motives. Be kind anyway. If you are successful, you will win some unfaithful friends and some genuine enemies. Succeed anyway. If you are honest and sincere people may deceive you. Be honest and sincere anyway. What you spend years creating, others could destroy overnight. Create anyway. If you find serenity and happiness, some may be jealous. Be happy anyway. The good you do today, will often be forgotten. Do good anyway. Give the best you have, and it will never be enough. Give your best anyway. In the final analysis, it is between you and God. It was never between you and them anyway."

Mother Teresa

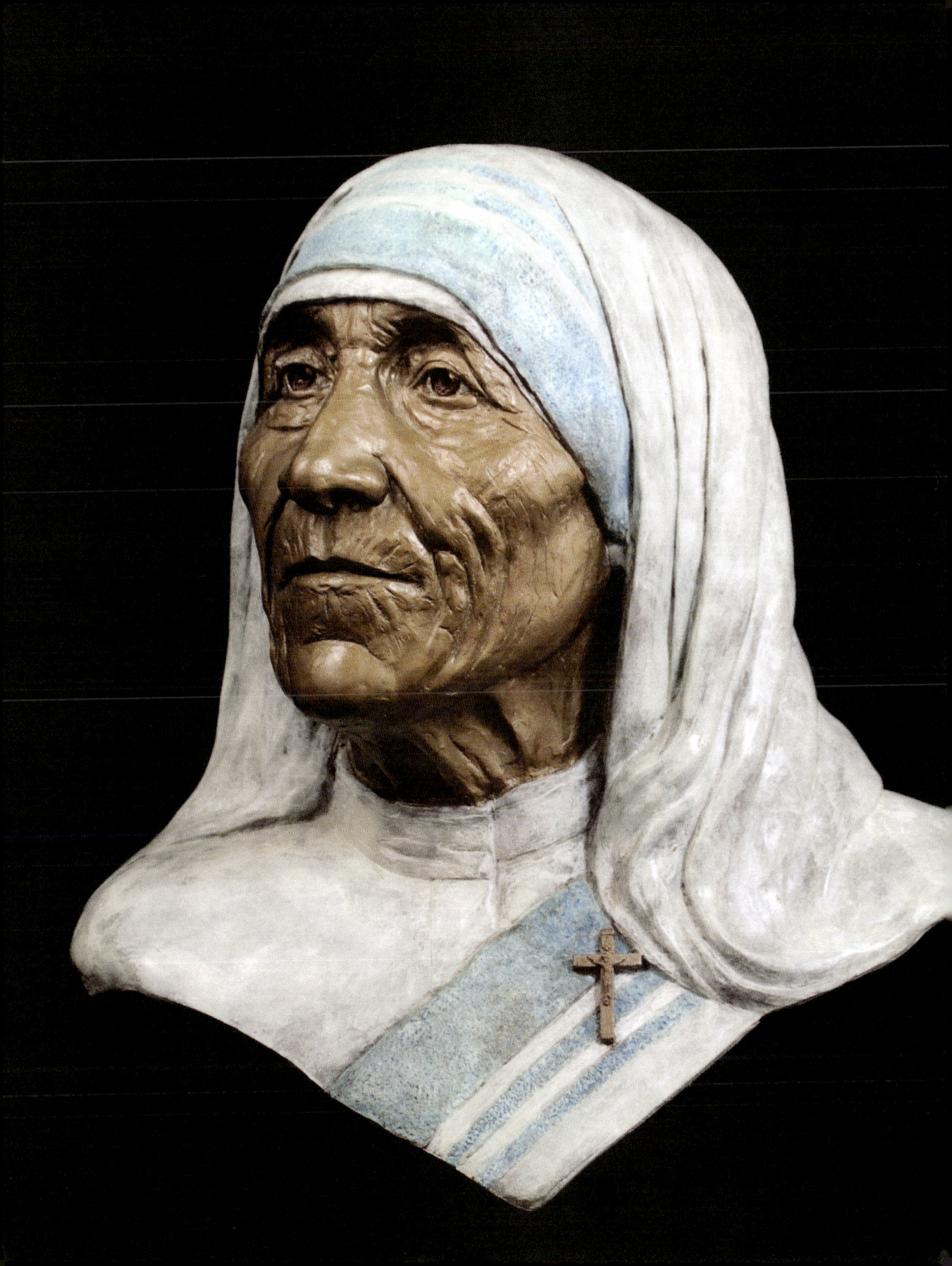

Chief Joseph Hinmatoowyalahtq'it 1840-1904

My next sculpture was of Chief Joseph of the Nez Perce, who was loved, respected, and reputed as a supremely honorable man. The story of Chief Joseph and his tribe is a horrific one. Like so many during that time they suffered severe injustice from the American government, but under very difficult circumstances, the peaceful Nez Perce did the best they could to strive for justice.

"If the white man wants to live in peace with the Indian he can live in peace. There need be no trouble. Treat all men alike. Give them the same law. Give them all an even chance to live and grow. This earth is the Mother of all people, and all people should have equal rights upon it."

Chief Joseph

After the sculpture was completed I contacted the Nez Perce tribe and offered to donate a copy. Unknown to me, a visitor center was opening up on the Lolo Pass in Idaho, six weeks later. The tribe was delighted to receive this gift and place it in the new center. I brought the sculpture to the opening personally, and it was received with great joy. I had the opportunity to meet some important tribal members and descendants of Chief Joseph. The Lolo Pass Visitor Center has become a stopping place for adults and children to reflect on the story of the Nez Perce, and I am told by the Visitor Center staff that the sculpture is a favorite of visitors. Such a delight for me to hear! I chose to create his hair in partial braids and some long, as I read that this was what was done when someone was mourning. I also read that Chief Joseph died of a broken heart, which I considered mourning. I hope you will take a journey to the beautiful land of the Nez Perce (or as they call themselves, Nee-me-poo) in Northern Oregon, Washington, Idaho, and Montana.

Please take time to look at the recommended reading list at the end of this book. My favorite books were: *The Nez Perce Indians and the Opening of the Pacific Northwest* by Alvin M. Josephy, Jr. and *That All People May Be One People, Send Rain to Wash the Face of the Earth* by Chief Joseph. There are many more worth reading to honor and remember.

You may also learn more at **www.fs.fed.us/npnht**.

"I am tired of talk that comes to nothing. It makes my heart sick when I remember all of the good words and the broken promises. There has been too much talking by men who had no right to talk. Too many misrepresentations have been made; too many misunderstandings have come up between the white man and the Indians."

Chief Joseph

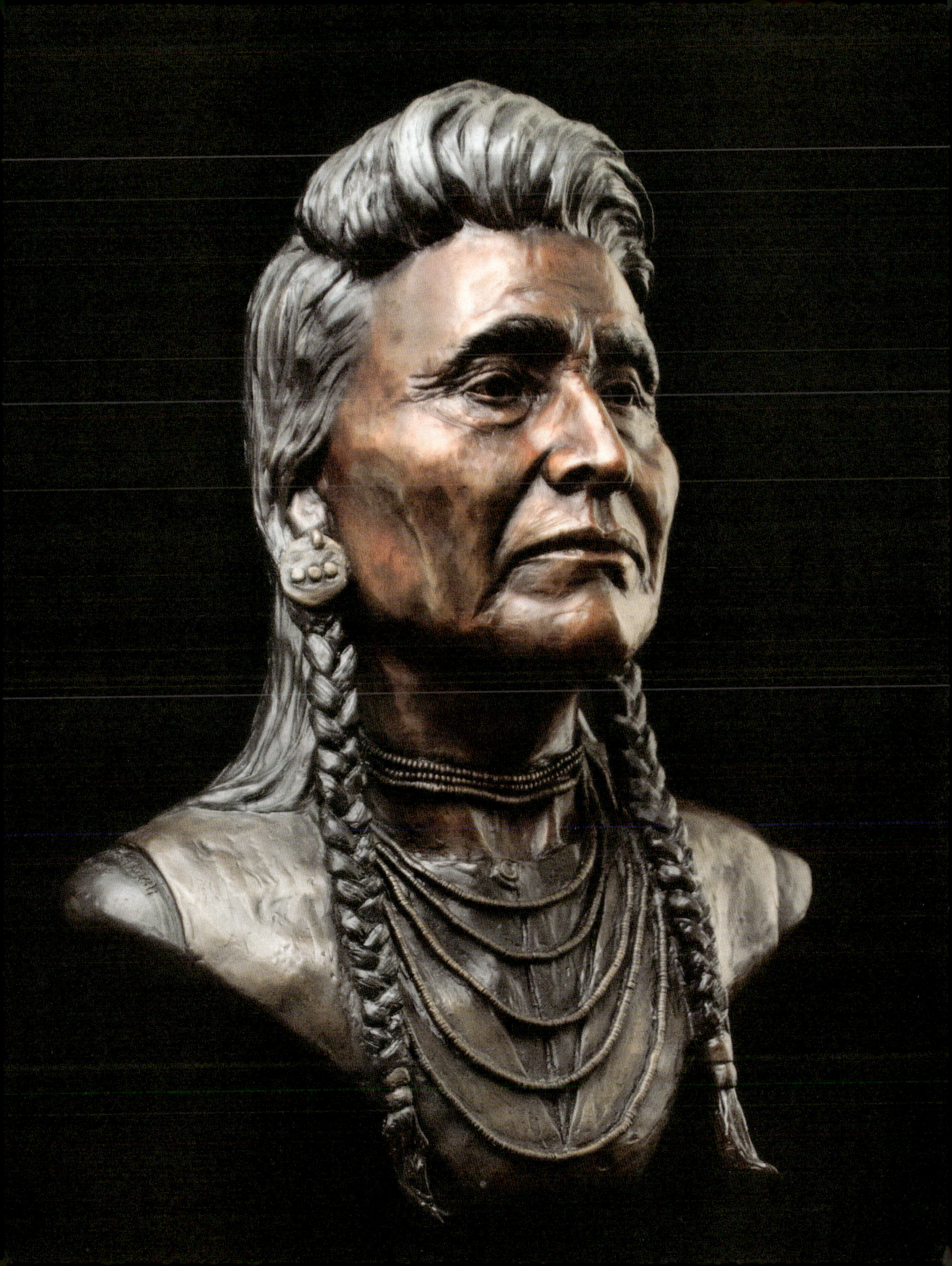

H.H. The Dalai Lama 1935-

I read the autobiography of the Dalai Lama, spiritual leader of Tibet, and learned of the violence and trauma his country went through. Knowing of his compassionate commitment to nonviolence, the Dalai Lama seemed like the natural next choice. Even in the midst of trauma, he has maintained an open compassionate heart, and encourages others to do the same. Time and again, the Dalai Lama has stressed the need for an end to violence between nations and a commitment to world peace. This is the desire of millions. It is no wonder that he has become a cherished speaker around the world. His website is **www.dalailama.com**.

"A good motivation is what is needed: compassion without dogmatism, without complicated philosophy; just understanding that others are human brothers and sisters, and respecting their human rights and dignities. That we humans can help each other is one of our unique human capacities."

HH the Dalai Lama

Because of his troubling circumstances, more people know of the Dalai Lama and his spiritual path than ever before. Life has a way of bringing us challenges we would never choose, but in the end, these challenges, though trying, often have a hidden gift we did not expect.

I sculpted His Holiness with a broad smile. Most sculptors do not like to sculpt smiles or teeth, but this was, to me, a necessary feature; it is befitting that his countenance is one of joy. I also added a colored patina to the sculpture to represent the colors he always wears.

"I believe that the very purpose of life is to be happy. From the very core of our being, we desire contentment. In my own limited experience I have found that the more we care for the happiness of others, the greater is our own sense of well-being. Cultivating a close, warmhearted feeling for others automatically puts the mind at ease. It helps remove whatever fears or insecurities we may have and gives us the strength to cope with any obstacles we encounter. It is the principal source of success in life. Since we are not solely material creatures, it is a mistake to place all our hopes for happiness on external development alone. The key is to develop inner peace."

"Happiness is not something ready made. It comes from your own actions."

HH the Dalai Lama

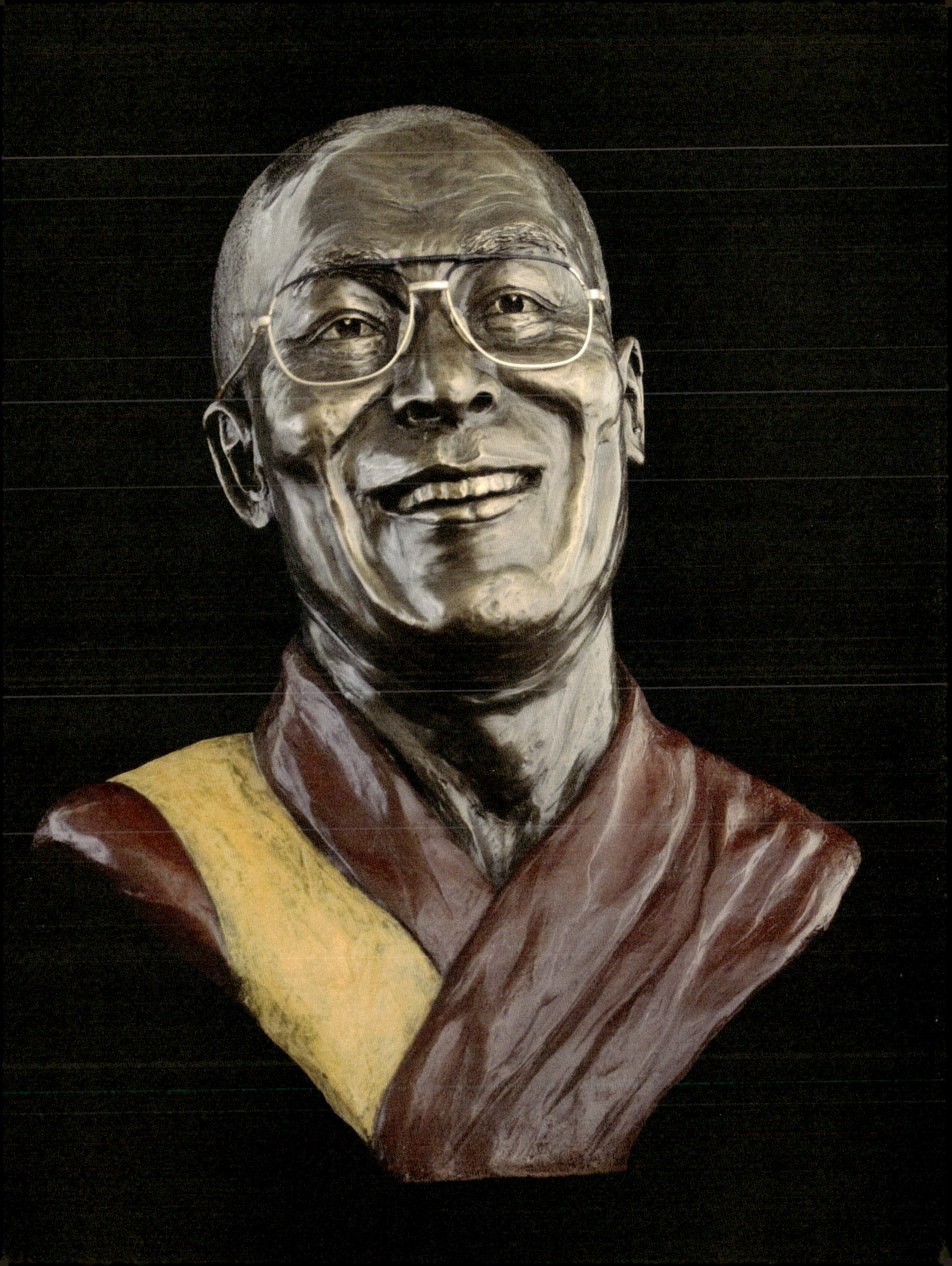

Cesar Chavez 1927-1993

Cesar Chavez, born in the United States with Mexican heritage, was not only inspired by Gandhi but also committed his life to following Gandhi's methods. He completely embraced the cause of nonviolent action in working for the benefit of his fellow farm workers.

This quote from Chavez exemplifies his philosophy:

> *Nonviolence is a very powerful weapon. Most people don't understand the power of nonviolence and tend to be amazed by the whole idea. Those who have been involved in bringing about change and see the difference between violence and non-violence are firmly committed to a lifetime of non-violence, not because it is easy or because it is cowardly, but because it is an effective and very powerful way.*

"It is possible to become discouraged about the injustice we see everywhere. But God did not promise us that the world would be humane and just. He gives us the gift of life and allows us to choose the way we will use our limited time on earth. It is an awesome opportunity."

Cesar Chavez

I have read much about this remarkable man and learned many things that helped me create this sculpture. I not only discovered his passion for his cause, I also discovered some personal things about him; That Chavez frequently wore a favorite leather jacket with a pin created by the United Farm Workers. He also had a special shirt that he was fond of which his mother gave him. So I chose to sculpt Chavez wearing that shirt, jacket, and pin. It was my way to connect with, not just the humanitarian, but also the man who loved his family. Chavez' family chose to sacrifice much during his time of service, as have the families of many great peacemakers. That type of loving support is one of the essential keys to their success.

Visit to learn more: **www.cesarechavezfoundation.org**.

"We cannot seek achievement for ourselves and forget about progress and prosperity for our community... Our ambitions must be broad enough to include the aspirations and needs of others, for their sakes and for our own."

Cesar Chavez

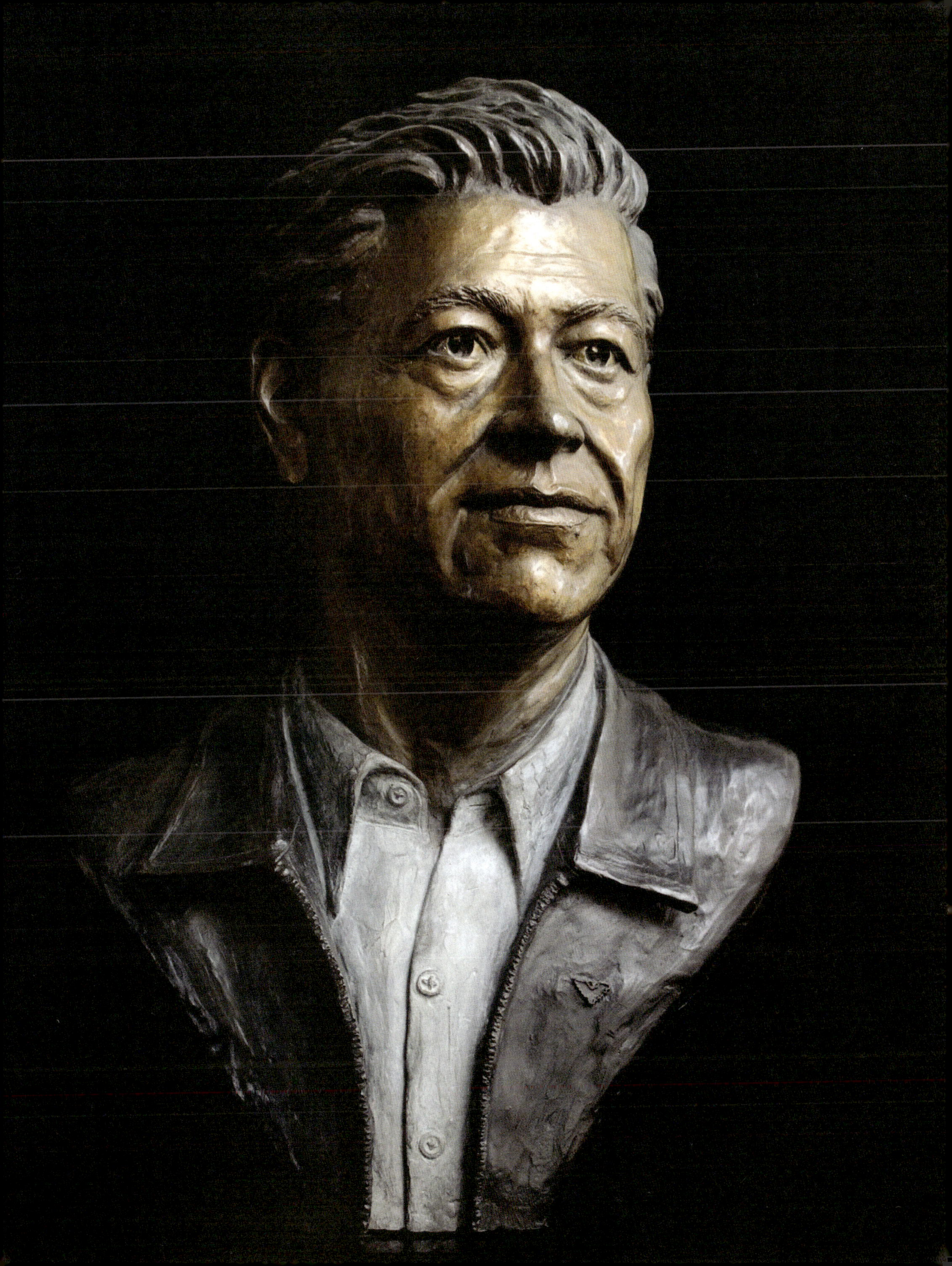

Danilo Dolci "The Gandhi of Sicily" 1924-1997

In one of my foundry classes, I met a man from Sicily. I told him I was sculpting a series of people that had been inspired by Gandhi. "Oh," he said, "How about Danilo Dolci? He was called 'The Gandhi of Sicily.'"

I had never heard of Dolci, so with that trusted recommendation I read *Fire Under the Ashes: The Life of Danilo Dolci* by James McNeish. It had an immediate impact on me. I wondered why I had never heard about this amazing man and his life. Here, I thought, was a monumental story to share; his was a life of untiring dedication to the poor of Sicily and to nonviolent action. Dolci is a humanitarian in the highest sense. He was nominated for the Nobel Prize in Literature and wrote many books about his work. *The World is One Creature* is one of my favorites.

"It is senseless to speak of optimism or pessimism. The only important thing to remember is that if one works well in a potato field, the potatoes will grow. If one works well among people, they will grow. That's reality. The rest is smoke."

Danilo Dolci

I wrote to the Dolci Trust, an organization maintaining his work and honoring his life, to offer them a copy of the Dolci sculpture. Eventually I received a wonderful reply: "We are so delighted to get this email. We have wanted a sculpture of Dolci for many years, but have not been able to acquire one. Will you come to Sicily as our guest at the celebration of his coming to our town 50 years ago?" What an opportunity!

It was 2002 when I completed the sculpture, and unbeknownst to me, just in time for the 50th anniversary celebration in Trappeto, Sicily, honoring Dolci's arrival to their town. I traveled to Trappeto, and the night I arrived I met my thoughtful host Vito La Fata, who had been trained by Dolci and now runs www.cesie.org, an organization inspired by the life and work of Danilo Dolci. Vito took the sculpture to the home of a dying man who had always dreamed of having a sculpture of Danilo Dolci for the town. When the dying man saw the sculpture, I was told he wept with joy. I met Dolci's children, sister and friends; saw the school he created and much more. This was a powerful and unexpected experience. It is unheard of for an American to take sculpture to Italy. It was meant to be. Who knew?

Dolci wore rimless glasses, so, to create the illusion of that, I made partial glasses and added bits of shiny bronze under the eyes to mimic the reflection of glass. Stand back and take a look, and hopefully you will see that illusion.

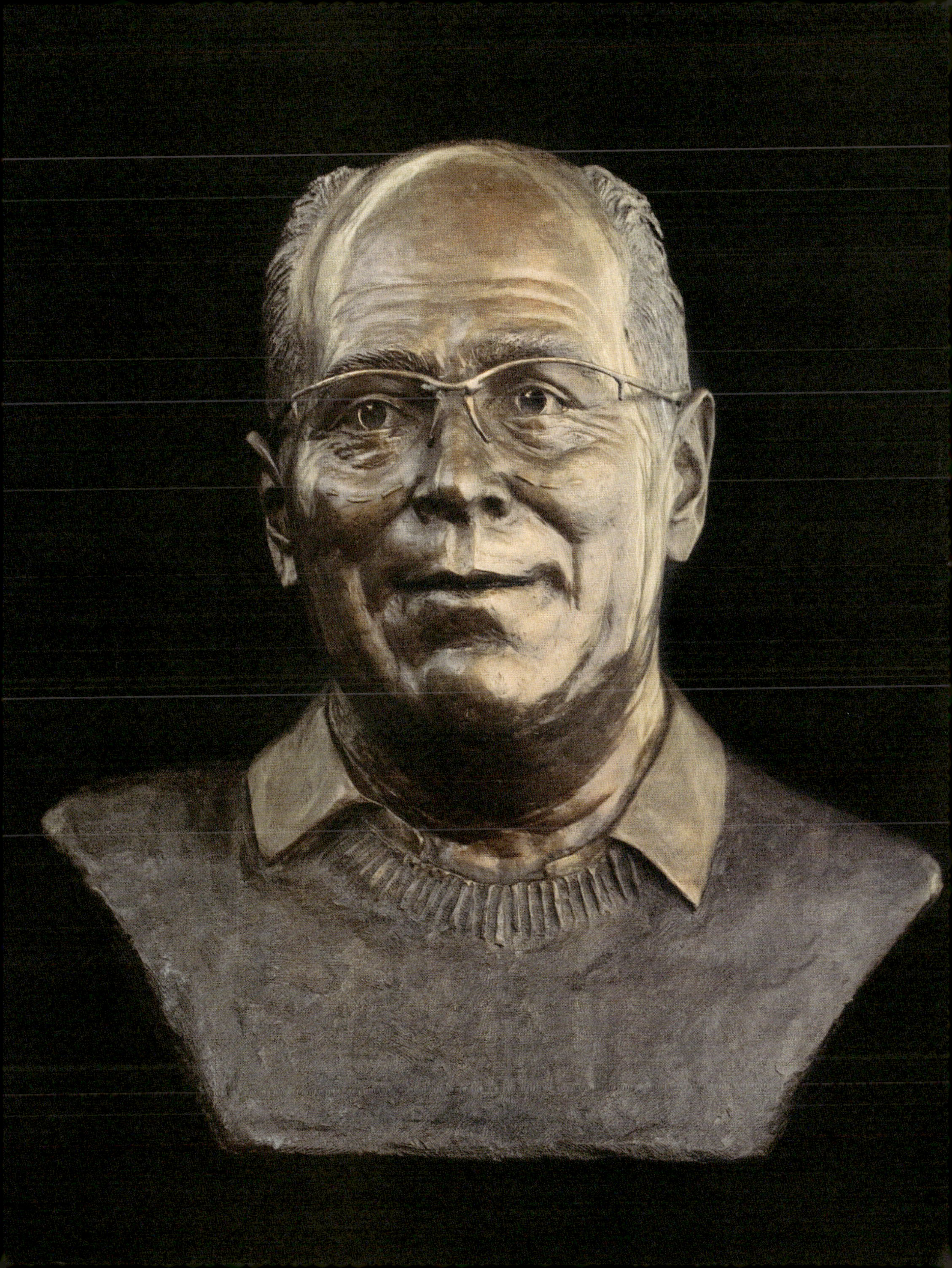

Meena 1956-1987

I unexpectedly received a call from an old high school friend, Joan. Knowing of my project, she told me about a book she had just read about an incredible woman named Meena. The book was *Meena: Heroine of Afghanistan* by Melody Chavis. I read it and immediately knew Meena would be my next sculpture.

If you are concerned about terrorism, hatred, and mistreatment of women, or wish for a deeper understanding of the courageous women of Afghanistan, this is the book to read. As the founder of Revolutionary Association for the Women of Afghanistan, the first human rights organization for women in Afghanistan, Meena is a perfect model for public service. Her sacrifice for others was the utmost: her life.

I was deeply touched by Meena's story and the women who have followed in her footsteps. I created this sculpture to honor her memory and the women of RAWA. I wrote to RAWA and informed them I would be making a sculpture of Meena for my series. Very swiftly, I received a reply with approval. They sent me photos of Meena to work from, and I sent back photos of my progress. When the sculpture was finished, I emailed a final picture of the bronze. Their response was fantastic, an email written in huge letters that read, "WONDERFUL, LOVE, KISSES AND HUGS for your great work. We are speechless."

It has been most rewarding bringing Meena's story to the attention of others, notably the OHSU School of Nursing at Southern Oregon University which invited me to talk about Meena's work creating desperately needed hospitals in Afghanistan. From that visit many nursing students read her book. Can you imagine my delight and amazement at how these sculptures bless my life with joy and gratitude? Not only for the lives of the people I am sculpting, but also the impact, and inspiration their lives and stories continue to have.

In the Meena sculpture, you will notice a slight raise in her right shoulder. In the main photo I chose to replicate, she has her arm raised in a victory salute. Sadly, it would have been too costly to create the entire gesture, so I ask you to try to imagine that victory salute.

Visit **www.rawa.org** to learn much more.

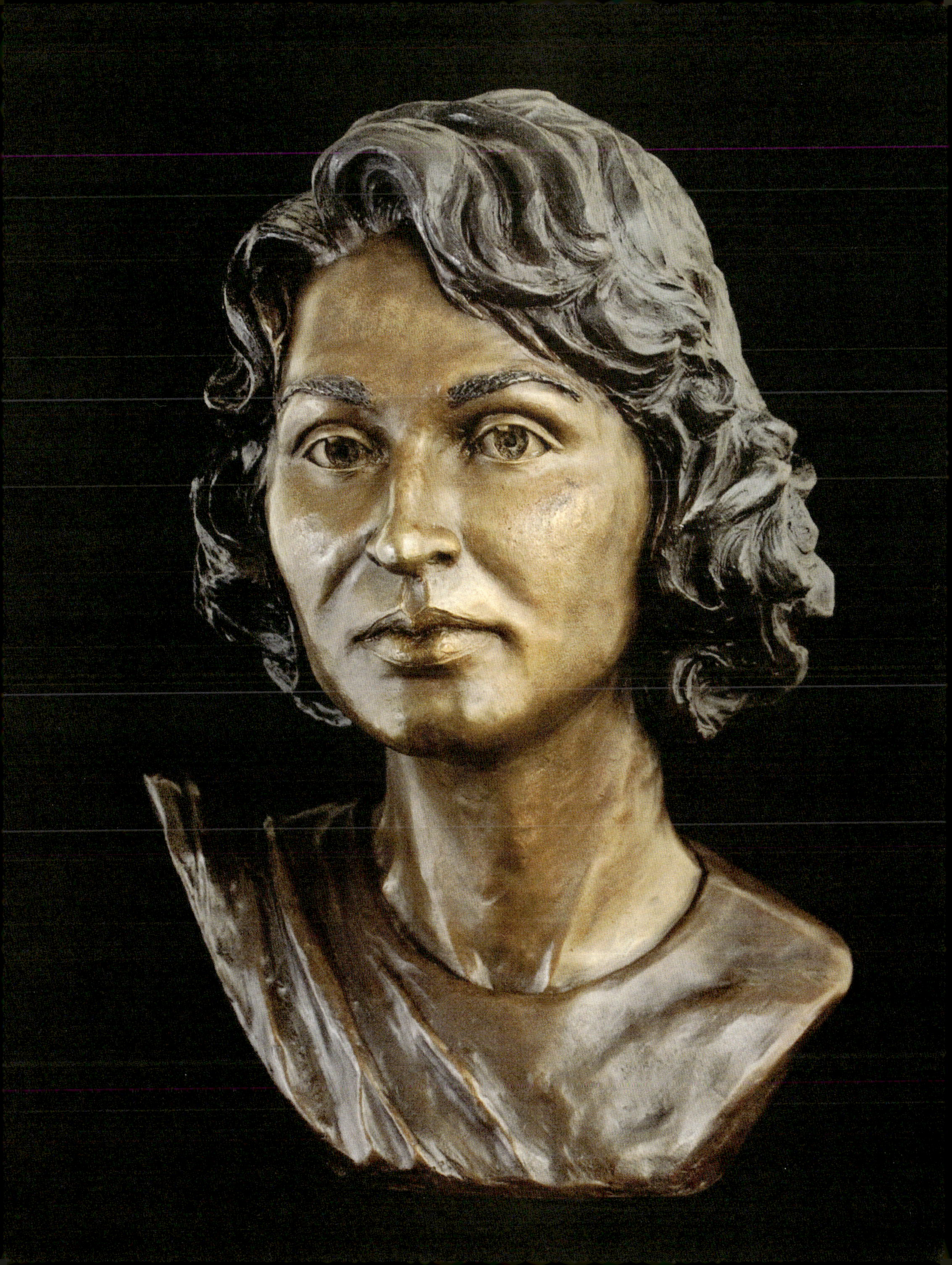

Peter Benenson 1921-2005

After my visit to Sicily I traveled Italy for another two weeks through SERVAS.org and met a lovely couple that had worked as volunteers for Amnesty International for many years. I told them I was looking for subjects from different countries and cultures for my series, and they suggested Peter Benenson, founder of Amnesty International. Benenson allowed me to represent another new country, England. Thank you, Patricia and Walter (and, of course, your daughter for giving up her room for me. Your hospitality was superb, your suggestion was brilliant.

When it was time to start sculpting, my mentor, Christopher Pardell, said, "Meera, you need to work smaller. If you want to continue this series, you will need to make some money to continue." He also pointed out that most people can't afford—nor particularly want—a life-size sculpture in their homes. Therefore, working with harder plastiline clay, I decided to sculpt on a smaller scale. I display the sculpture of Benenson with a candle wrapped in barbed wire, the symbol for Amnesty International.

www.amnestyinternational.org

"On May 28 1961 I wrote an article in The Observer newspaper which gave birth to Amnesty International. It began with these words: Open your newspaper any day of the week and you will find a report form somewhere in the world of someone being imprisoned, tortured or executed because his opinions or religion are unacceptable to his government. The newspaper reader feels a sickening sense of impotence. Yet if these feelings of disgust could be united into common action, something effective could be done. Pressure of opinion a hundred years ago brought about the emancipation of the slaves. Pressure of opinion is now needed to help Amnesty International achieve its ultimate objective: to close for business. Only then, when the last prisoner of conscience has been freed, when the last torture chamber has been closed, when the United Nations Universal Declaration of Human Rights is a reality for the world's people, will our work be done."

Peter Benenson

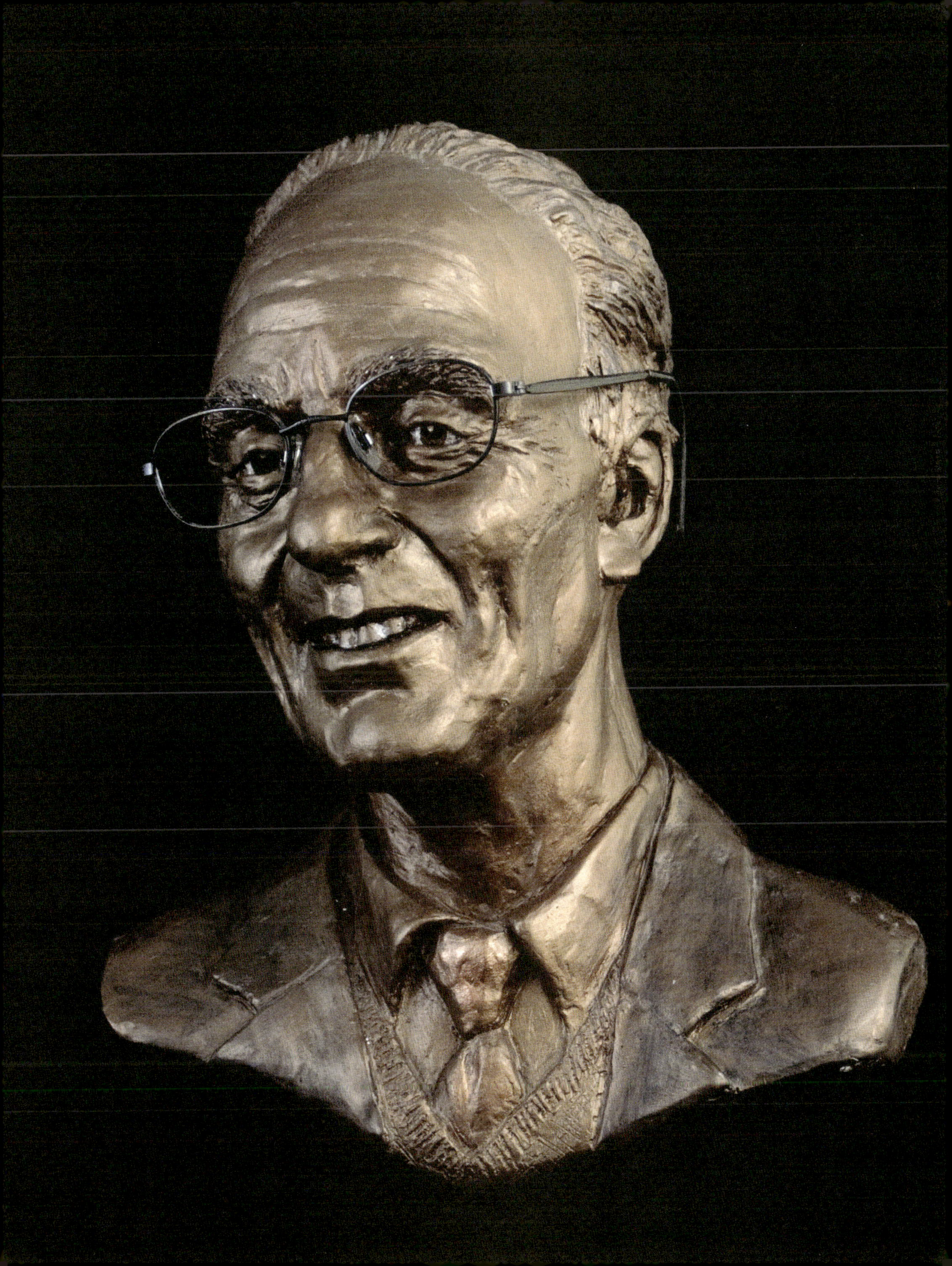

Mairead Corrigan McGuire 1944-
Betty Williams 1943-

Now, for practical purposes, I continued working on a smaller scale. The next country I chose to represent was Ireland to tell the story of the Peace People founders, Mairead Corrigan Maguire and Betty Williams, is heart-wrenching: Mairead's sister, Annie, was walking down a street with her three children. An IRA bomber driving by was shot by British police. The car went out of control and hit the family. Annie was pinned to a fence with a broken pelvis and two broken legs. Her children were killed in front of her.

I can't help wondering why it takes such violence to mobilize for change, but in this case, it certainly did. Maguire and Williams organized a movement, the Peace People, to stand up to the violence that had been tearing Ireland apart for years, with some help from Ciaran McKeown. Through group marches thousands, made up mostly of women, Maguire and Williams, led a stand for Peace. They marched with Catholic and Protestant women, a controversial act at that time. Despite threats and harassment, they all stood together for a common cause. In time, their untiring efforts decreased the violence in Ireland by fifty percent, earning these two women the Nobel Peace Prize in 1976.

"All of need to take responsibility for the world's violence and, like Gandhi, pledge our lives to the nonviolent transformation of the world in order to resolve these insane cries through the wisdom of nonviolence."

Mairead Corrigan Maguire

The story of the Peace People is one that could be told in many countries today. I hope that, in reading about them, you will find inspiration towards some type of action—to speak out and to help others living in violent conditions. Please learn more about this heartbreaking story and of how it changed the lives of thousands through the dedication of this group.

www.peacepeople.com

"God doesn't start wars. That's the greatest load of nonsense. Mankind starts wars. But then we bless armies to go and kill in God's name. Somebody's got to blow that myth out of the water."

Betty Williams

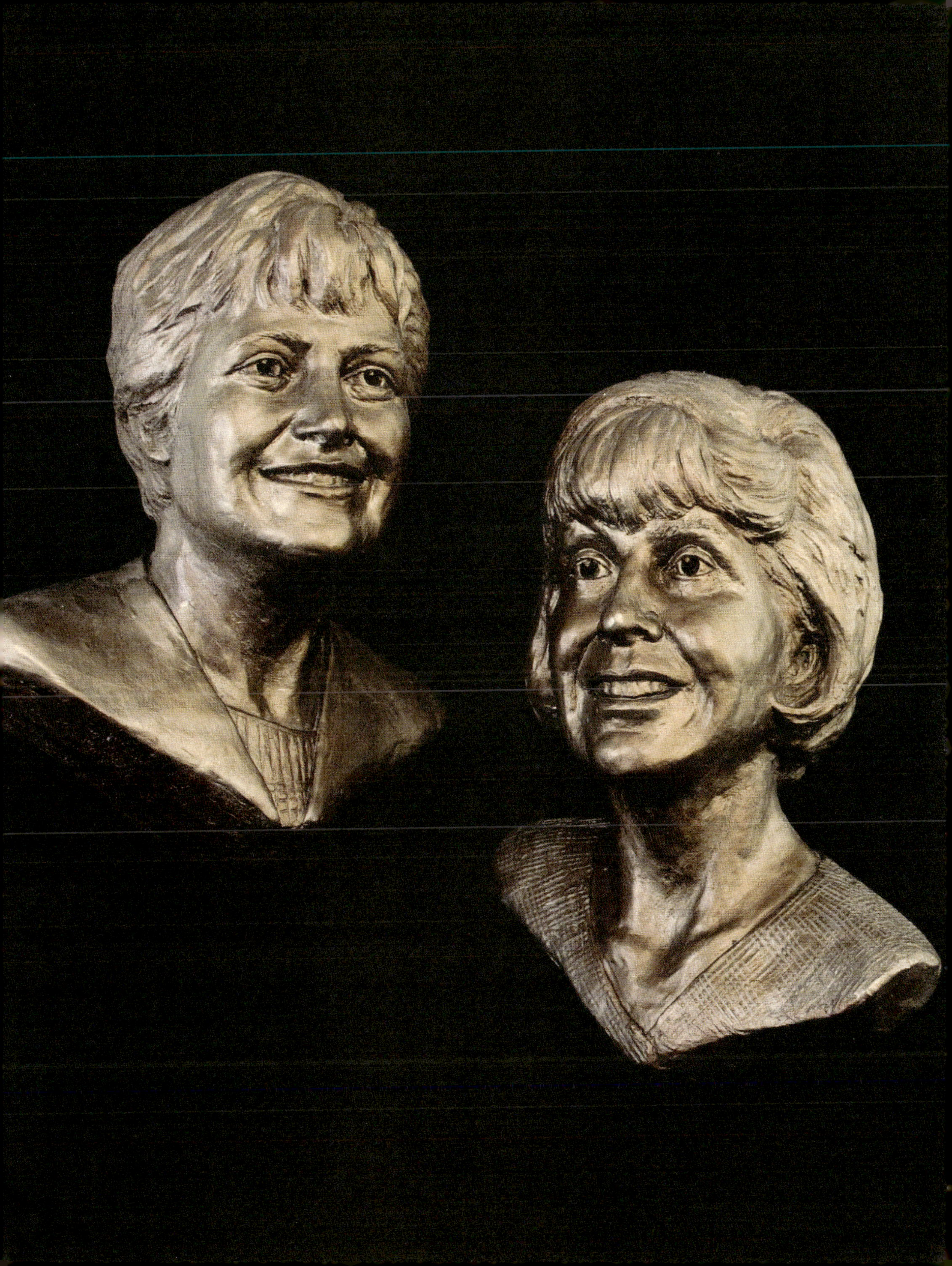

Albert Schweitzer 1875-1965

Dr. Albert Schweitzer had great foresight in planning his life. He studied to become an accomplished musician, earning doctorate degrees in music, theology, and philosophy, yet still managed to fulfill his required military training. At thirty, while still in school, he decided to study medicine and dedicate the rest of his life to serving humanity. After graduating from medical school, he created the Albert Schweitzer Hospital in Gabon, Africa.

"The scientist should not live for science alone, nor the businessman for his business, nor the artist for his art. If affirmation of life is genuine, it will demand from all that they should sacrifice a portion of their own lives for others."

Albert Schweitzer

Dr. Schweitzer's story may leave you inspired just by knowing a man lived with such depth of spirit. His commitment to live with "Reverence for all Life" in these days of environmental breakdown is a timely reminder worth pondering daily. His example can teach us much about the rewards and joys of service.

Schweitzer's autobiography, a best seller in its time, is called *Out of my Life and Thought*. You can also learn more about this man and his work at **www.schweitzerfellowship.org**.

"I knew that a system of values which concerns itself only with our relationship to other people is incomplete and therefore lacking in power for good. Only by means of reverence for life can we establish a spiritual and humane relationship with both people and all living creatures within our reach. Only in this fashion can we avoid harming others, and, within the limits our capacity, go to their aid whenever they need us."

Albert Schweitzer

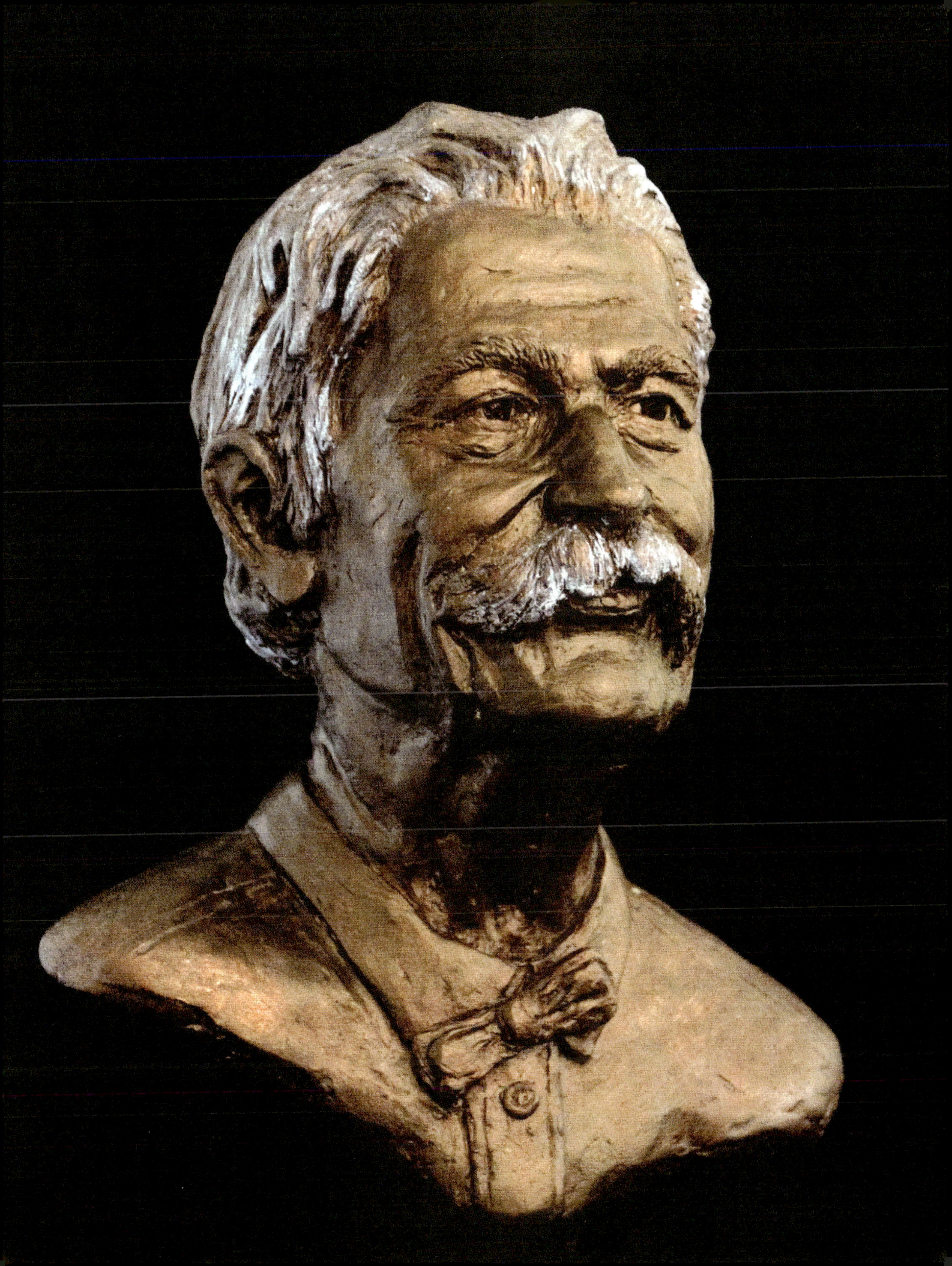

Dr. Marshall Rosenberg 1934-

Dr. Marshall Rosenberg is the founder of the Center for Nonviolent Communication. I met him through Annie Muller, a dear friend of my husband. Marshall has played a special role, in not only my life but also the lives of hundreds of thousands around the globe. He has traveled around the world for over forty years sharing the tools for nonviolence through communication. His book, *Nonviolent Communication: A Language of Life,* which is dedicated to Annie. My husband, Alex, and I took several of Marshall's classes; over the years, we have found his methods to be invaluable to both our personal relationships and our internal dialogs—how we speak to ourselves to serve life, by making our choices based on what brings us joy, rather than "I should, or I have to do something." NVC brings our awareness to the value of our choices so we tell ourselves, "I choose to do this because..." Different energy.

"Don't fill the air with a lot of words. Rather, create a flow where the other person can tell you what they need to know."

Dr. Marshall Rosenberg

Alex is still a Certified Trainer, and although I was at the time, I chose to take time off in order to work on this series. I cannot imagine living without these tools:

Empathetically listening: observations, feelings, needs, requests
Honestly expressing: observations, feelings, needs, requests

Sounds very simple. However, this philosophy calls for observation without evaluation, owned feelings, basic human needs, and realistic doable requests. These teachings also address what Marshall considers the true, basic human needs: acceptance, affection, security, stability, and authenticity, among others. These tenets teach us to give from the heart, never from a *should*, *ought to*, or *have to*. Simple? It takes true commitment to live this way, but the rewards are well worth the effort.

I highly encourage you to check out the Center for Nonviolent Communication's website, **www.cnvc.org**. And read Marshall's most valuable book which has been translated into over twenty languages to date.

"What I want in my life is compassion, a flow between myself and others based on a mutual giving from the heart."

Dr. Marshall Rosenberg

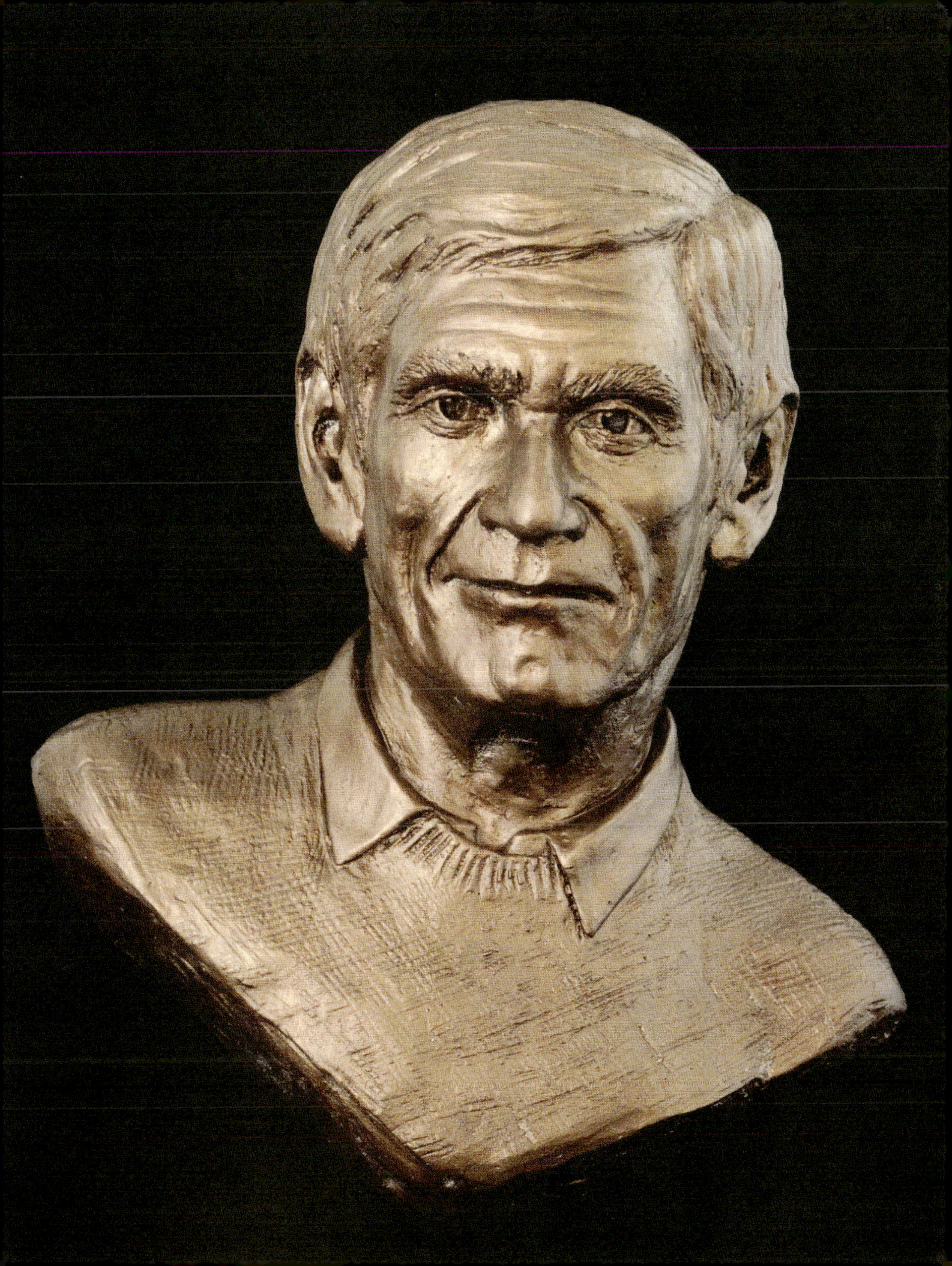

Albert Einstein 1879-1955

Albert Einstein is renowned for many scientific breakthroughs, less so for his statements on nonviolence found in many inspiring quotes. Creating this sculpture came from reading about how Einstein and other scientists spoke out against using the atom bomb on Japan. They were convinced that a demonstration of the bomb's power, without damage to human life, would be sufficiently effective. They, of course, were not successful in their protest, but they did their best to stop this horror.

"Any intelligent fool can make things bigger, more complex, and more violent. It takes a touch of genius—and a lot of courage—to move in the opposite direction."

Albert Einstein

Einstein was no stranger to the ugly side of discrimination, and he rejected biased attitudes. His words, often uplifting and thoughtful, prompted me to add him to this series.

Learn more at **www.Nobelprize.org**.

"Human beings are a part of a whole called by us the 'Universe', a part limited in time and space. We experience ourselves, our thoughts and feelings, as something separated from the rest—a kind of optical delusion of consciousness. This delusion is a kind of prison for us, restricting us to our personal desires and to affection for a few persons nearest to us. Our task must be to free ourselves from this prison by widening our circles of compassion to embrace all living creatures and the whole of nature in its beauty."

"Peace cannot be kept by force. It can only be achieved by understanding."

"We can't solve problems by using the same kind of thinking we used when we created them."

Albert Einstein

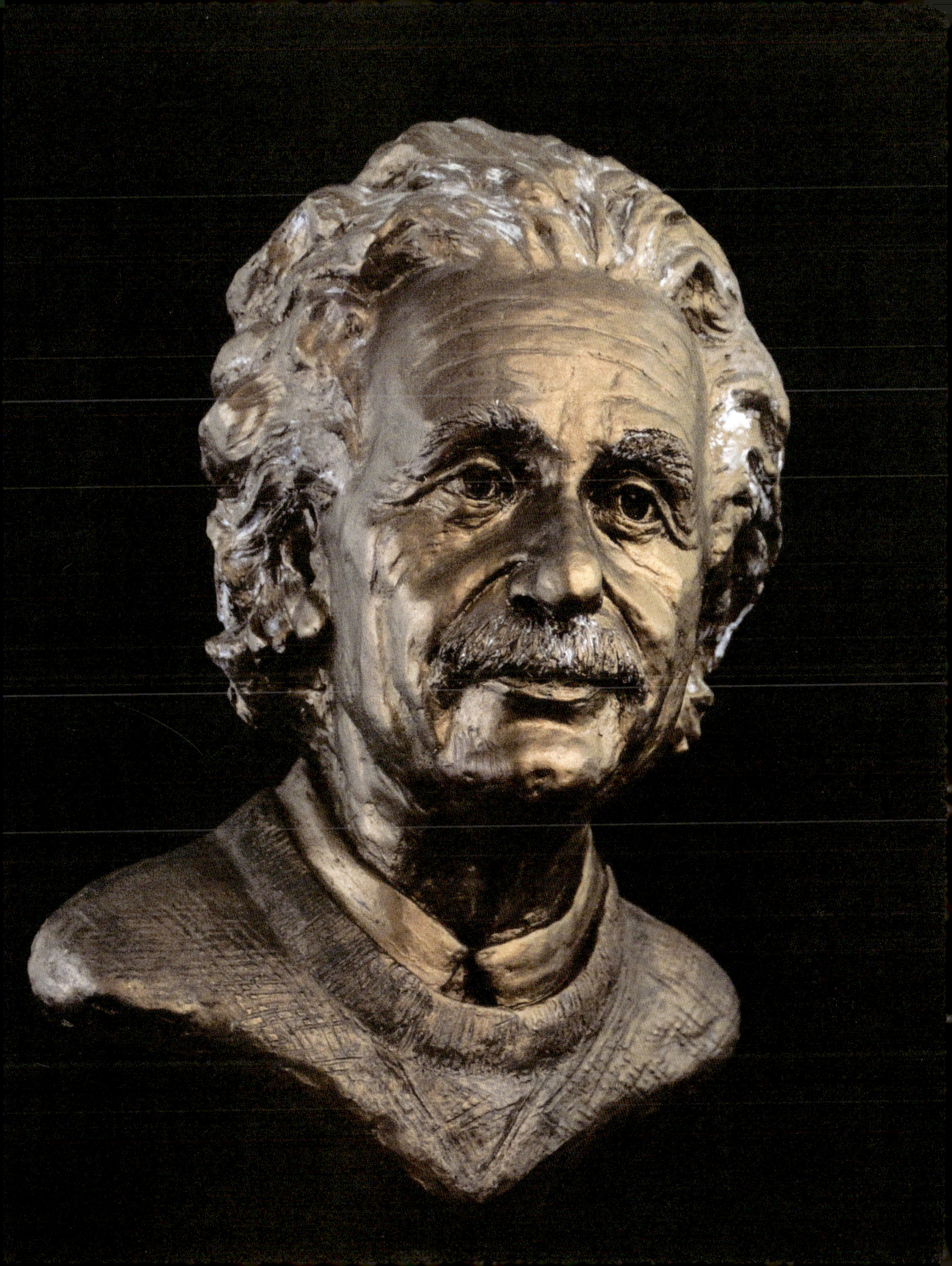

John Muir 1838-1914

John Muir was the co-founder and first president of the Sierra Club. He has a fascinating life story which he has written about in *The Story of My Boyhood and Youth*, as well as many other books. He did not work for nonviolent social change in the usual ways, but I believe his dedication to saving environmental beauty merits adding his life to this series of humanitarians. Beautiful places of nature are often sources of peace and improved spirit. John Muir's wisdom and vision for preserving these places is a nonviolent contribution that will benefit generations to come.

"When one tugs at a single thing in nature, he finds it attached to the rest of the world."

John Muir

His life was fascinating, and his life accomplishments were many. The book, *John Muir: Nature Writings: The Story of My Boyhood and Youth; My First Summer in the Sierra; The Mountains of California; Stickeen; Essays*, tells much of that fascinating life. He wrote many books—much to choose from to learn what adventures the love of nature can bring into a life.

Two informative websites are **www.johnmuir.org** and **www.sierraclub.org**. They continue to do marvelous work, you might enjoy checking them out.

"Everybody needs beauty as well as bread, places to play in and pray in where nature may heal and cheer and give strength to the body and soul."

"In every walk with nature one receives far more than he seeks."

"Climb the mountains and get their good tidings. Nature's peace will flow into you as sunshine flows into trees. The winds will blow their own freshness into you, and the storms their energy, while cares will drop off like autumn leaves."

"Keep close to Nature's heart...and break clear away, once in awhile, and climb a mountain or spend a week in the woods. Wash your spirit clean."

John Muir

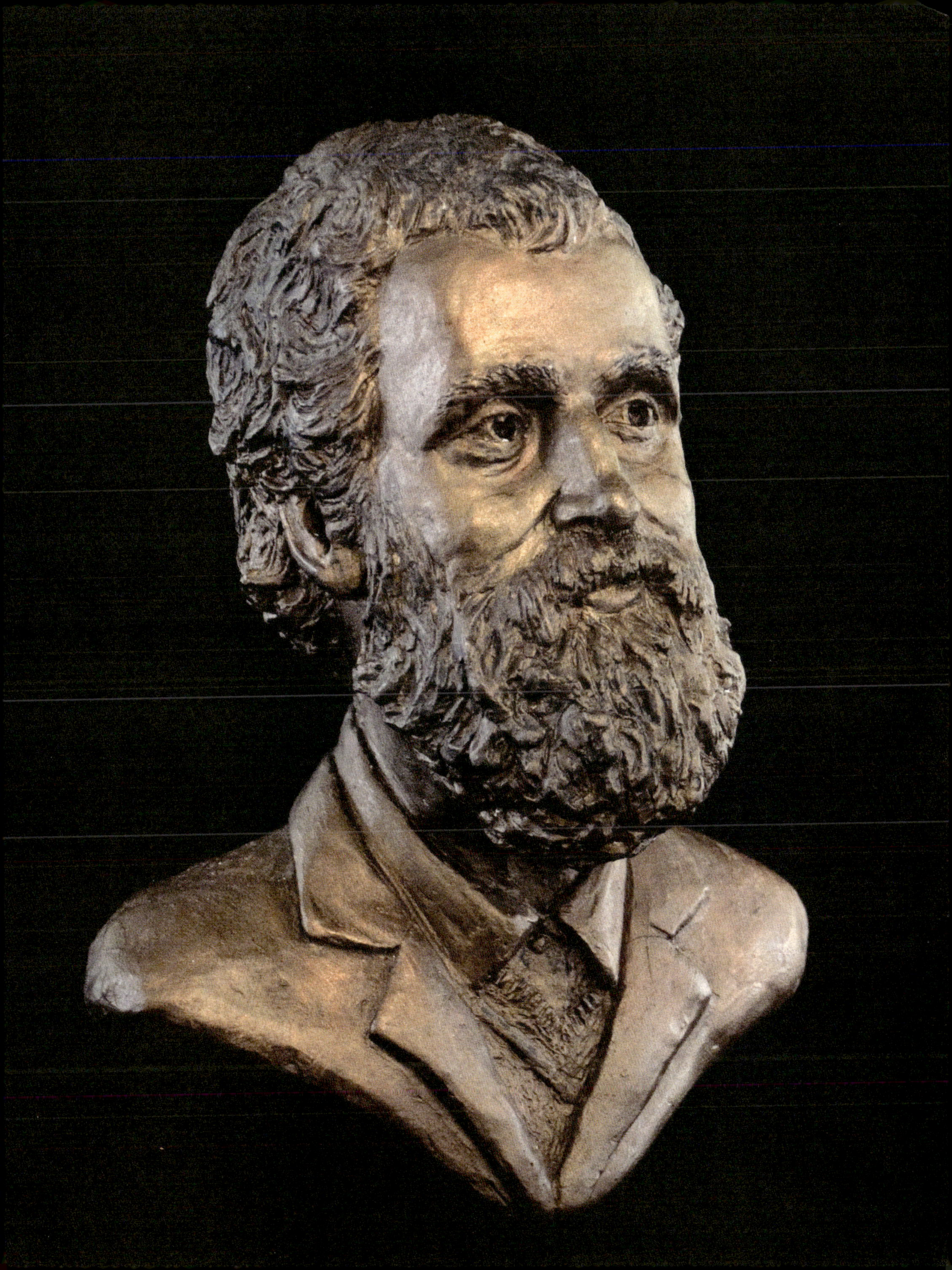

Nelson Mandela 1918-
Desmond Tutu 1931-

Nelson Mandela and Desmond Tutu have lived for a passionate cause—freedom from apartheid. I dearly wanted to add them both to this series because of their deep understanding that violence is not the answer to the long-term need of people living together respectfully and harmoniously. Mandela's autobiography, *The Long Road to Freedom*, gives insight into Mandela's life and his commitment to humanitarian work. The life of Desmond Tutu shows a true understanding of what it takes to make real social changes in the midst of very difficult circumstances.

"Our greatest glory consists not in never falling, but in rising every time we fall."

Nelson Mandela

The struggle for change was long and tiresome, with twenty seven years of imprisonment for Mandela, and constant work by Tutu, and many others, to keep up the struggle for justice and peace. In the end, their efforts brought freedom and humanitarian shift in a country ravaged by apartheid. Without their constant vigilance, this terrible circumstance could have been much more horrifying. But with wisdom, insight, and dedication over long years, change did occur.

The sculptures depict Mandela and Tutu together on Inauguration Day, a victory for them, all the blacks of South Africa, and many supporters around the globe—a time of great rejoicing.

"A good head and a good heart are always a formidable combination."

Nelson Mandela www.nelsonmandela.org

"The only thing necessary for the triumph [of evil] is for good men to do nothing. If you are neutral in situations of injustice, you have chosen the side of the oppressor."

Archbishop Desmond Tutu www.tutu.org

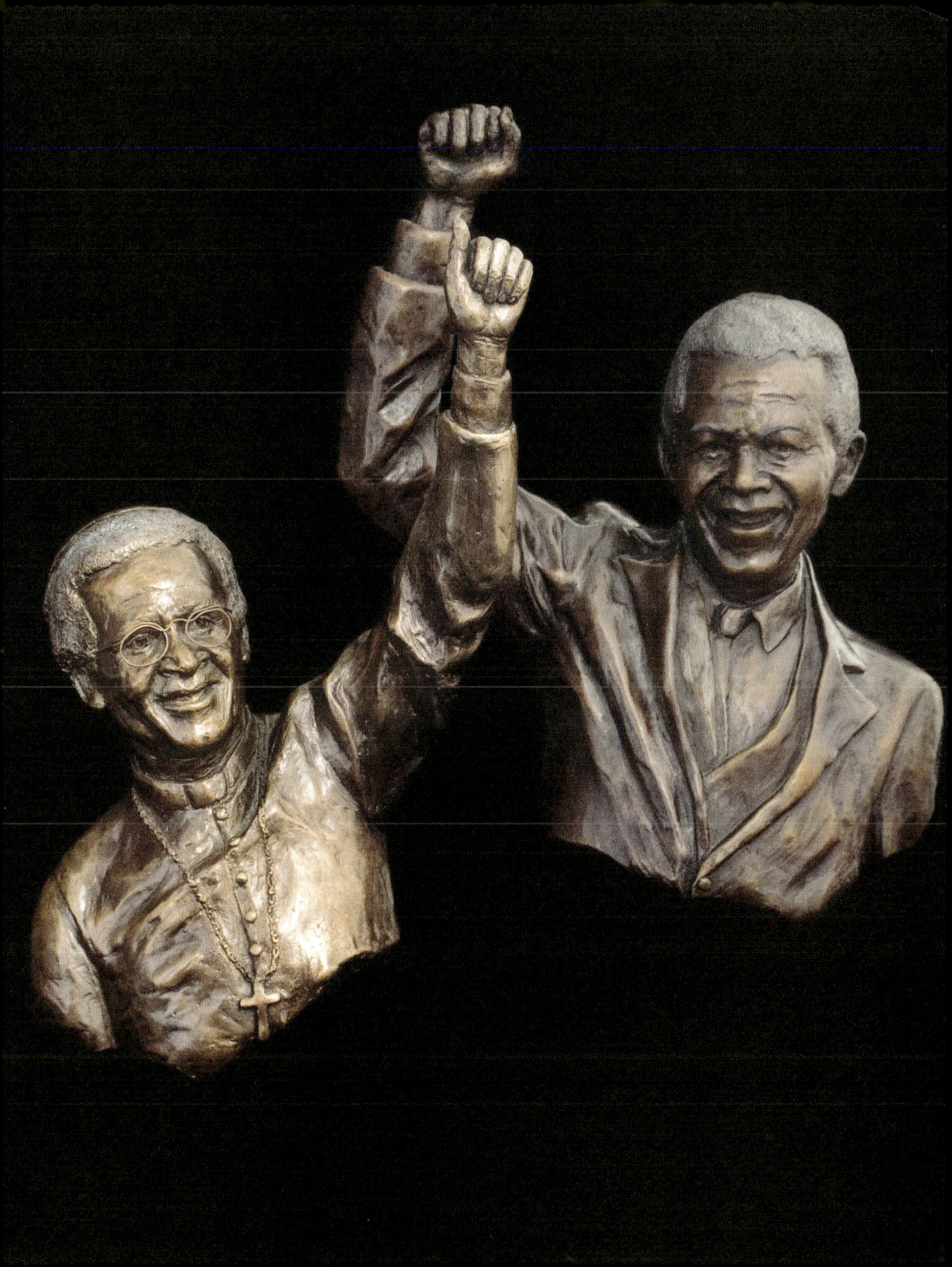

Sister Chan Khong 1938-

Choosing Sister Chan Khong for this series came unexpectedly. There is a notable Vietnamese population in Southern California, so I wanted to sculpt someone from that culture, particularly for the interest of Vietnamese schoolchildren. My choice was Thich Nhat Hahn, a nominee for the Nobel Peace Prize. However, when I went to see him at his Deer Park Monastery, a mishap had me arriving too early.

"If we just worry about the big picture, we are powerless. So my secret is to start right away doing whatever little work I can do. I try to give joy to one person in the morning, and remove the suffering of one person in the afternoon. If you and your friends do not despise the small work, a million people will remove a lot of suffering."

Sister Chan Khong

While waiting for the meeting, I took the opportunity to visit the monastery's bookstore. There, I came across the book *Learning True Love: How I Practiced Nonviolent Social Change* by Sister Chan Khong. She has since changed the title. After reading the Sister Chan Khong's book, it became clear to me that her story needed to be told. Happily, both she and Thich Nhat Hahn liked my idea to add a sculpture of her to the series.

I believe that this sculpture carries the energy of her dedication to others, energy that has weathered much adversity but has grown from deep compassion. Her book tells of her nonviolent humanitarian work under extremely violent conditions and of how she managed to keep an open, compassionate heart, in spite of it all. She continues her humanitarian work to this day.

"For Sister Chan Khong [True Emptiness] working for social change and helping people are sources of joy for her. The love and concern that underlie her work are deep. True Emptiness is also true love. Her story is more than just the words. Her whole life is a dharma talk."

Thich Nhat Hanh

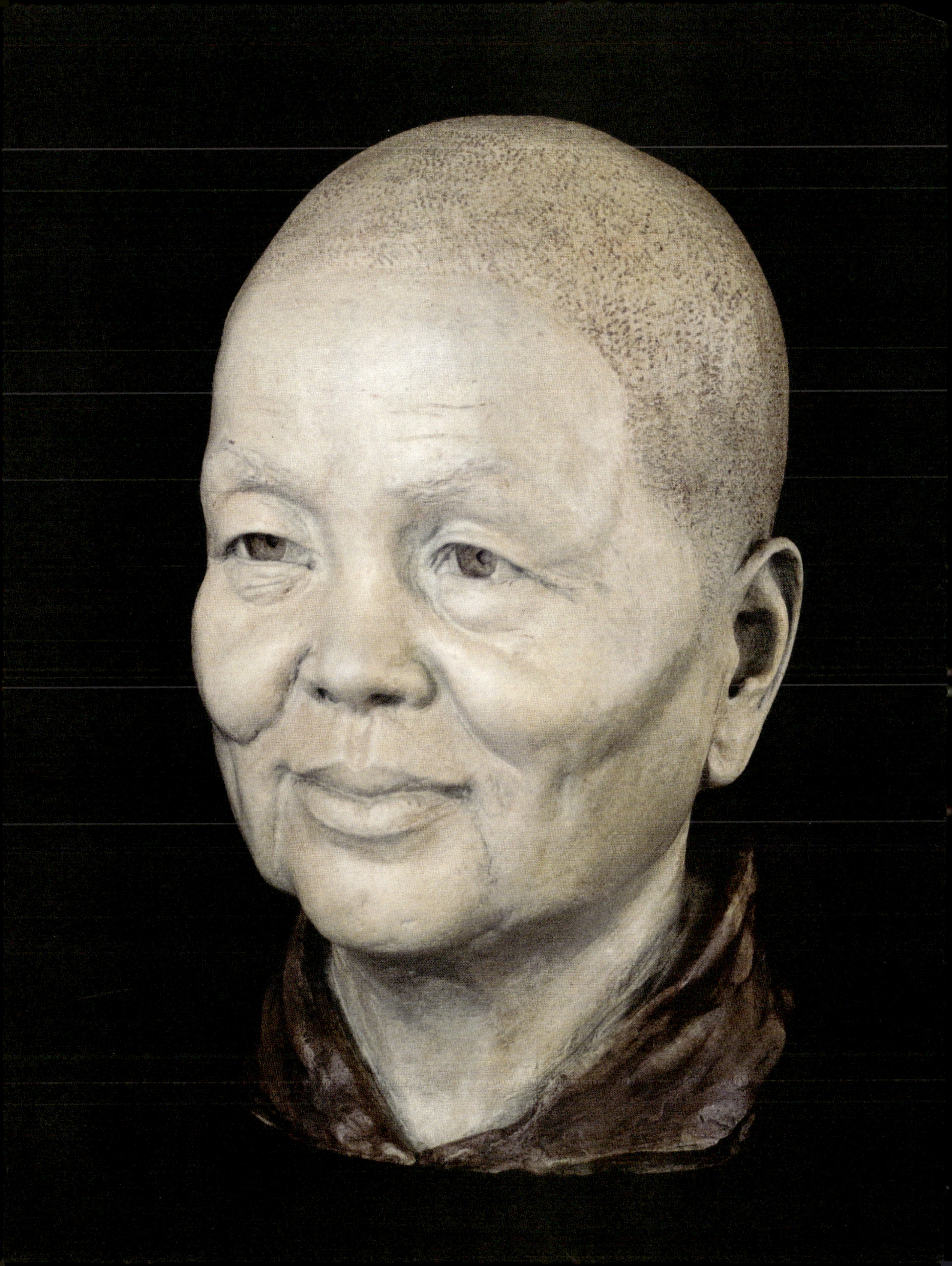

Tariq Khamisa 1975-1995

I heard about the Tariq Khamisa Foundation from a friend who knew of my sculpture series and recommended I read Azim Khamisa's book, *Azim's Bardo: From Murder to Forgiveness a Father's Journey*. It is one of the most powerful stories I know of that demonstrates true forgiveness in difficult circumstances. Khamisa's personal journey took place following the murder of his only son, Tariq, by a fourteen-year old gang member. This tragedy led to an extraordinary act of forgiveness, and the founding of the Tariq Khamisa Foundation. Azim and Ples Felix the grandfather of the boy who murdered Tariq, made the decision to start an organization that educates children at risk for gang violence. They teach about nonviolent alternatives and about the pain families go through because of personal loss, in what they call their "Violence Prevention Forum." They speak to over 18,000 schoolchildren a year and have won many awards for their tireless work. Please learn more at **www.tkf.org.**

"I will mourn Tariq's death for the rest of my life. Now, however, grief has been transformed into a powerful commitment to change. Change is urgently needed in a society where children kill children."

Azim Khamisa

I had a difficult time deciding who in this story to sculpt. It would be natural to honor Azim Khamisa and Ples Felix, but ultimately I chose Tariq—the precious son whose life was lost. I later learned that the Muslim faith doesn't allow sculpture. Please forgive me and my ignorance if you are a Muslim. I believe that my sculptures are to remind us of the stories of true compassion at the heart of all faiths, that we all stand in awe of our creator and realize a Love that unites us, the place where compassion originates.

"The United States is arguably the greatest of all nations. But a child is arrested here for a violent crime every five minutes. Guns on the streets of the United States take the life of one of our youths every hour and a half. It chilled me to think of how many parents were wearing the same cloak of grief I was. Where were our priorities? We have such wealth, such ability, such achievement. Each week we push back daunting frontiers, we look to the ends of the universe through our telescopes. We stretch technology to communicate instantaneously anywhere in the world. We penetrate the secrets of the atom, the depths of the ocean. We design and build massive construction projects in miraculous time frames. We transplant organs and end Cold Wars. With some readjustment in priorities, couldn't we add, 'stop kids from killing other kids' to our impressive list of accomplishments? Wouldn't it be worth trying?"

Azim Khamisa

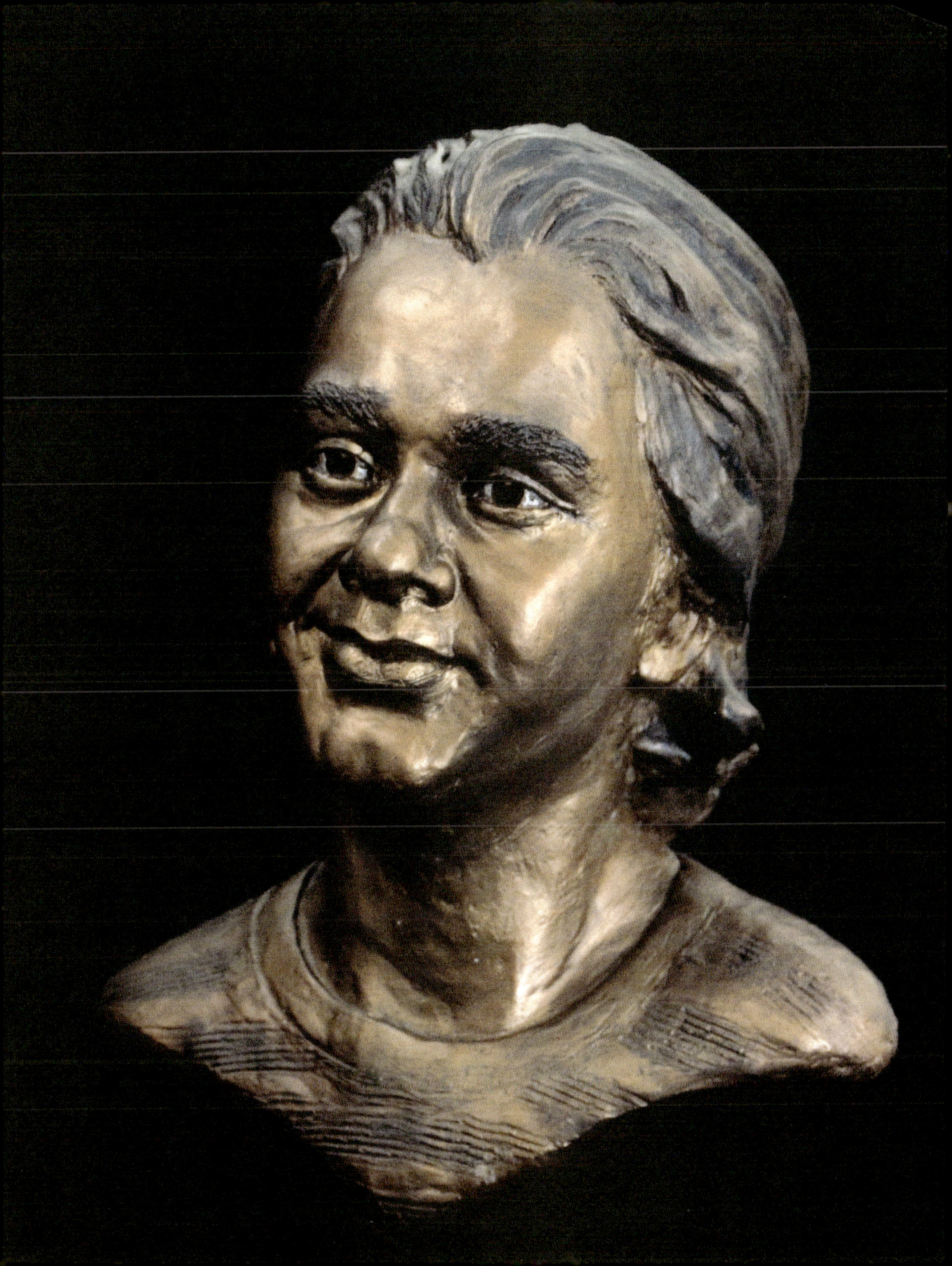

Mothers of the Plaza de Mayo

The Mothers of the Plaza de Mayo formed during *The Dirty War*, a seven-year period of state-sponsored violence when thousands of people were abducted by the Argentine government. The Mothers started with fourteen women who donned scarves, embroidered with the names of their "disappeared" children, and met each week in the Plaza de Mayo. Walking in a circle of silence, they strengthened the protest for many with missing family members. Longing to know why their children disappeared, their walking was in tribute to their children while risking their own lives in protest. Their action was powerful and unique. The Mothers continue today to help many in South America.

"We think that to be able to tell the truth, as difficult as it might be, to be able to face the powerful without violence, to face them as we do, gives us strength, a different kind of power, and not their kind."

Mothers of the Plaza de Mayo

I was moved to create this sculpture to honor this bravery and draw attention to their story, which has much to say of value to us all today. There are many websites and books about their unique way to draw attention to the need for justice, as well as a moving documentary, *Las Madres de la Plaza de Mayo*. When you read this story, you will be struck by their immense courage and their way of drawing attention to this circumstance without aggression. Since there were fourteen women in the founding group, I created my first bas relief of those women. The one in the center of the sculpture is Azucena, one of the fourteen founding Mothers who lost their lives for the protest, and the date she disappeared.

"This meant transforming anguish into action with a universal voice, a demand not only about the search for their children but for the rights of all human beings. Today we know that those kerchiefs in the street stopped the disappearances and there are many Argentineans who owe their lives to these Mothers circling the Plaza de Mayo."

Antonio Elio Brailovsky

"Now I know that we have to speak out about the injustices publicly. If not, we are accomplices. I am going to denounce them publicly without fear. This is what I learned. This is the form the struggle takes."

Maria del Rosario de Cerruti

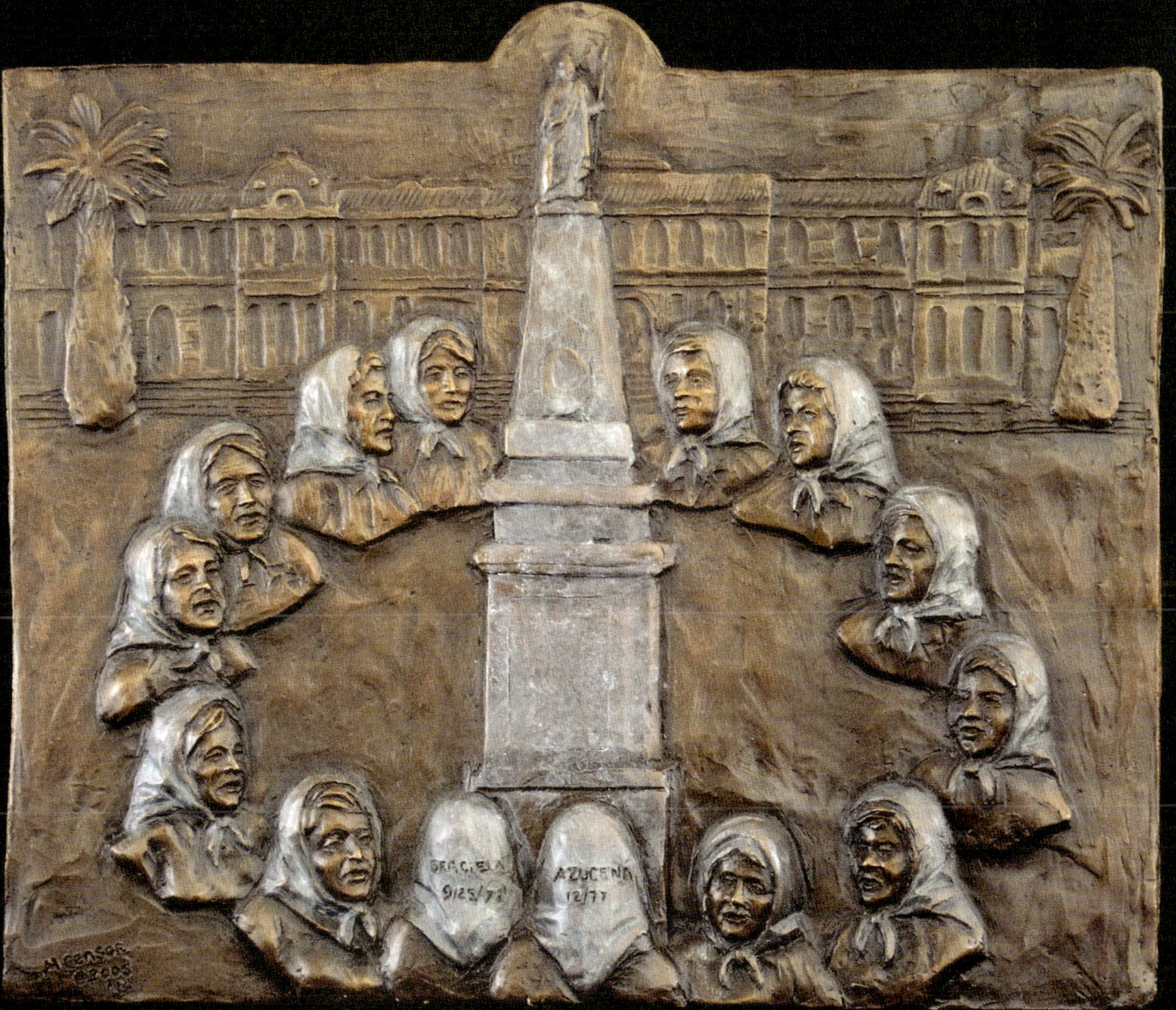
GRACIELA
9/25/77
AZUCENA
12/77

Father Gregory Boyle 1954-

I did say that I hope to create two more sculptures. Actually, there are thousands of people that I would like to represent, but two more is just about all that can fit into this collection.

"You stand with the least likely to succeed until success is succeeded by something more valuable: kinship. You stand with the belligerent, the surly, and the badly behaved until the bad behavior is recognized for the language it is: the vocabulary of the deeply wounded and of those whose burdens are more than they can bear."

from *Tattoos on the Heart*

I learned of Father Gregory Boyle and his work from my friend, Joe Sojka, and his daughter Jessica. Knowing of my interest in humanitarians, Joe took me to Homeboy Industries in Los Angeles. Homeboy Industries is the largest gang intervention and re-entry program in the county; it has become a national model for transforming lives and communities. "Jobs not Jails" is one of their mottos, along with "Nothing stops a bullet like a job."

At Homeboy Industries, I saw the radiant faces of ex-gang members who had turned their lives around. Knowing the dedication and commitment it took to get them there, I knew that Father Boyle, creator and mentor for Homeboy Industries, deserved a place in this series. By offering alternatives to gang violence, Father Boyle demonstrates true compassion in action.

Father Boyle is a true hero for many, including myself. I believe that he and his stories will certainly touch your heart. His book, *Tattoos on the Heart*, is a testament to the power of compassion. He is a wonderful writer; reading this book will be a pleasure that opens your heart wider… guaranteed. He says about the stories he tells: "With any luck, they will lift us up so we can see beyond the confines of the things that limit our view."

"Kindness is the only strength there is."

Father Gregory Boyle

This man lives a life of inspiration and commitment to others. He demonstrates compassion, a true life-changer. His smile tells it all. I deeply admire his work and hope that you will help support him by buying his book or donating to Homeboy Industries.

Visit Homeboy Industries at **www.homeboy-industries.org** to learn more of Father Boyle's work and of how ex-gang members have gone from violence to dignity, anger to kindness. You can also listen to his talks on YouTube.

"We are all more than the worst thing we have ever done."

Father Gregory Boyle (aka Father Greg, Father G, G-dog, or just G)

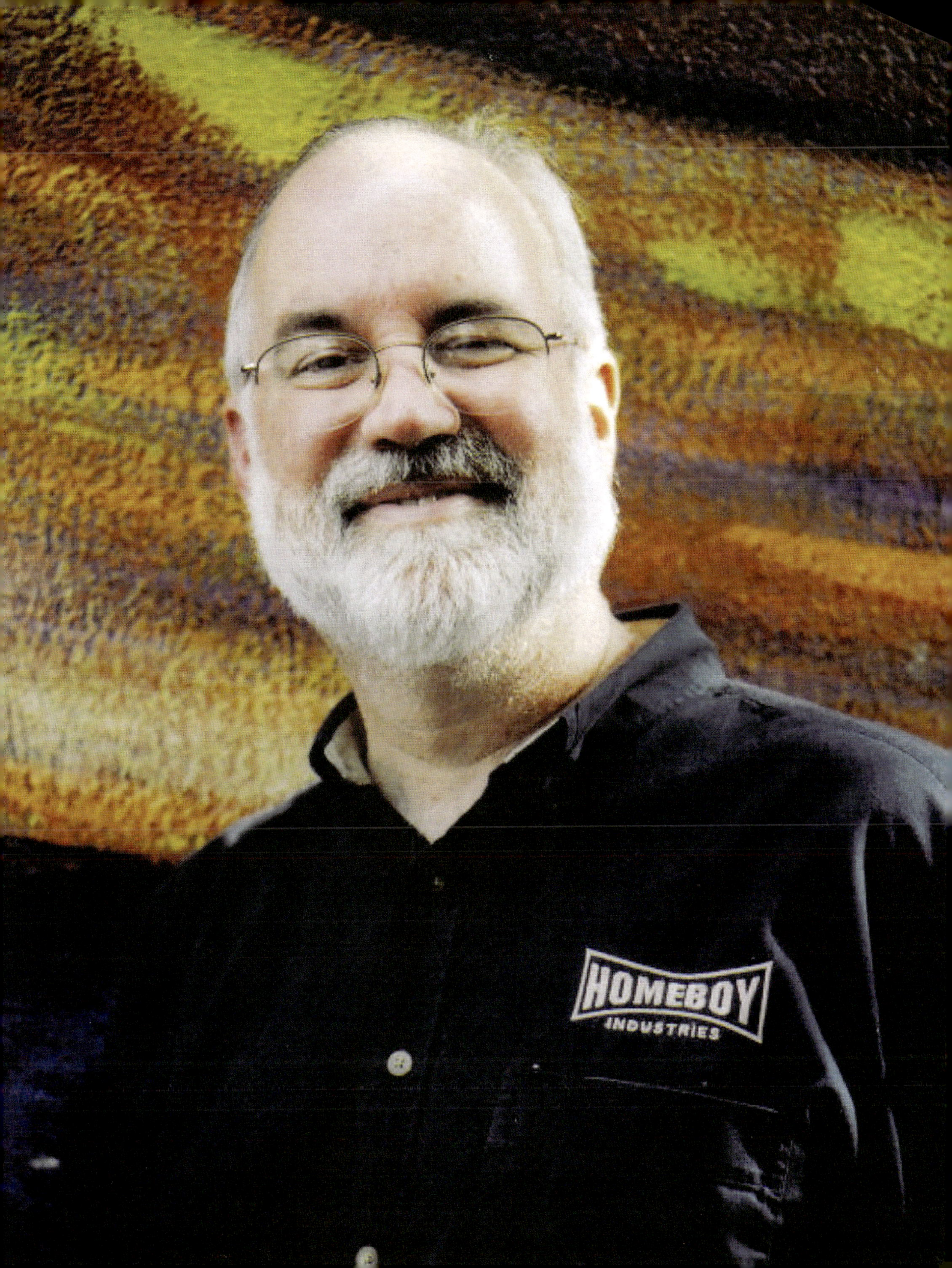
HOMEBOY
INDUSTRIES

Dr. Catherine Hamlin 1924-

The next and final person I have chosen is Dr. Catherine Hamlin. Dr. Catherine and her husband, Reginald Hamlin, founded a most important Fistula Hospital in Ethiopia, and they have trained many others to perform this life-changing surgery. Reginald has since passed away, but Catherine is still living and continues her work in the senior years of her life. This is truly a gift from her heart.

Dr. Catherine's book, *The Hospital by the River*, and *Catherine's Gift* by John Little may inspire you to start a little fund where nonessentials are forgotten and, instead, put that money aside to donate to the Fistula Foundation, supporting women in need. You can also "Adopt a Sister" and change a woman's life forever. Please go to **www.fistulafoundation.org** to learn more.

The Fistula Foundation has a marvelous, heart-touching DVD called *A Walk to Beautiful*. This video is available through Netflix and the Fistula Foundation's website. I encourage you to purchase it in support of their work as well as to learn more of their heartfelt service.

"The Mission of the Fistula Foundation is to raise awareness of and funding for fistula treatment, prevention and educational programs worldwide.

An obstetric fistula develops when blood supply to the tissues of the vagina and the bladder (and/or rectum) is cut off during prolonged obstructed labor. The tissues die and a hole forms through which urine and/or feces pass uncontrollably. Women who develop fistulas are often abandoned by their husbands, rejected by their communities, and forced to live an isolated existence.

Eradicated in western countries at the end of the 19th century when cesarean sections became widely available, obstetric fistula continues to plague women throughout the developing world. It is estimated that there are 100,000 new fistula cases each year, but the international capacity to treat fistula remains at only 6,500 per year. The United Nations Population Fund (UNFPA) estimates the world's population of fistula sufferers at more than two million."

The Fistula Foundation

I hope to raise funds to create these last two sculptures by sales of this book and, once that is accomplished, to divide any continued profits between the organizations I so admire.

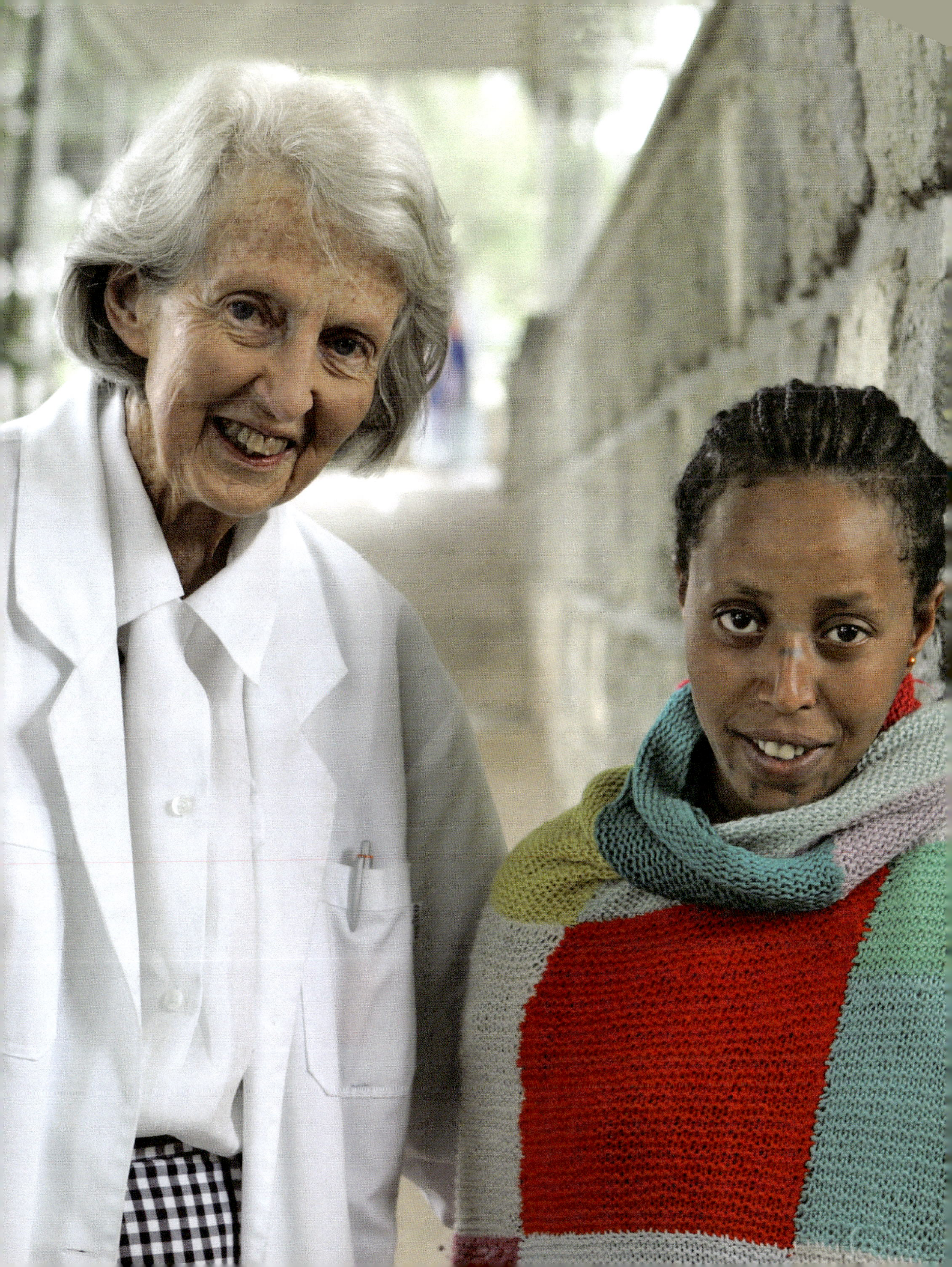

In Closing...

I feel blessed to have had the opportunity to create these sculptures, to share their stories with friends and family, to speak to hundreds of schoolchildren, and, of course, you. I hope you share my inspiration for change, peaceful action, compassion, and service from the heart. Please seek out more information about these incredible people and explore the possibility of what you can do and what is being done for nonviolent social change. There are four particular books I recommend:

A Force More Powerful: A Century of Non-Violent Conflict
by Peter Ackerman and Jack Duval

Good News for a Change: How Everyday People are Helping the Planet
by David Suzuki and Holley Dressel
This book is full of amazing and uplifting stories of people making wonderful and exciting changes for our environment.

How to Change the World: Social Entrepreneurs and the Power of New Ideas
by David Bornstein
Huge inspiration here, and fun to read, as well.

Is There No Other Way? The Search for a Nonviolent Future
by Michael N. Nagler
Much insight to the power of the experience of nonviolence.

I promise you these stories are worth the time it takes to read them, and they may truly give you new incentive to live in yet more ways that make a difference for future generations. They may also give you a great sense of gratitude for the human spirit that is acting with such beauty.

Below are a few more of my favorite quotes:

"These are the times when we stand humbly and boldly in the presence of our own great promise. These are the days when through our decisions and actions, we determine our legacy for those to come."
Jean Houston

"You make your own choices. Pick up the battle and make it a better world, just where you are. Yes, and it can be better and it must be better but it is up to us."
Maya Angelou

"Did you ever look at the problems of the world and say to yourself, 'How can I make a difference? There is so much need. How do I choose?' Well sometimes the problem chooses us. Sometimes the solutions choose us."

Turk Pipkin, www.nobelity.org, One Peace at a Time. A great DVD!

"The happiest people are the people who serve."

Wangari Maathai

For example: You could help save millions from injury and misery by learning how to help stop cluster bombing. These bombs look like toys on the ground and thousands of children have limbs blown off picking them up. Let's stop this.
www.stopclustermunitions.org

For another simple way to help the planet, check out **www.meatlessmonday.com/about**. Giving up eating meat for just one day a week removes 1.2 million tons of CO_2 from the atmosphere, saves 100 billion gallons of water, 70 million gallons of gas, 33 tons of antibiotics, 1.5 billion pounds of crops otherwise fed to livestock, and much more.

In May of 2011, this sculpture series has been placed in the Hannon Library at Southern Oregon University. I have also donated many of my books to the library, so they will be available to patrons and educators. Perhaps we will meet there someday. If you are looking for more information about this collection or the people represented in it, please visit my website. There you will find links to the various organizations I have mentioned, find your passion. Send your friends to visit the Hannon, purchase sculptures, or this book, or perhaps donate to the creation of the next two sculptures, or the organizations mentioned.

With any project, you meet people along the way who are invaluable help. In learning the sculpting process, mine were Christopher Pardell, Vladimir Medenica, Marsha Meers, and, most of all, Cicero D'Avilla, who invited me to his studio in Brazil as his guest and taught me how to refine my work. His art is exquisite and his generosity boundless. Timothy Nobles was a great resource for his book ideas. Lorraine Cook for the inspiration to get the whole series placed somewhere, and her invitation to speak to the nurse trainees. Paul Adalian for creating a team of support for me for placing the sculptures. Paul Chek and Penny Crozier for their celebration and support of my project. David Ruppe and Christy Collins for the layout of the book. A big thanks to Barb Barasa (websitings.net) who donated much of her time and talents to the creation of my website. Most importantly, I truly could not have done this series without my life partner, my dear husband Alex. Thank you for your love, support, and guidance. Whenever I felt like giving up on this project, you encouraged me to sleep on it and keep going. You are a huge blessing in my life.

With gratitude and joy,
The Unexpected Sculptor, Meera Censor

www.humanitariansculpture.com or **www.meeracensor.com**

Meera's Suggested Reading List

MAHATMA GANDHI

My Experiments with Truth by M.K. Gandhi
Gandhi the Man by Eknath Easwaran
The Words of Gandhi by Gandhi, Richard Attenborough, & Johanna McGeary
Nonviolent Soldier of Islam: Badshah Khan: A Man to Match his Mountains by Eknath Easwaran

MARTIN LUTHER KING, JR.

King Remembered by Flip Schulke & Penelope McPhee
Martin Luther King, Jr.: A Man Who Changed Things by Carol Greene

CESAR CHAVEZ

Conquering Goliath by Fred Ross
The Fight in the Fields by Susan Ferriss & Ricardo Sandoval

MOTHER TERESA

Something Beautiful for God by Malcolm Muggeridge
Mother Teresa: In My Own Words by Mother Teresa

SISTER CHAN KHONG

Learning True Love: How I Learned and Practiced Social Change in Vietnam by Sister Chan Khong

KASTURABAI GANDHI

Forgotten Woman by Sunanda & Arun Gandhi

CHIEF JOSEPH

The Nez Perce Indians and the Opening of the Northwest by Alvin M. Josephy
Chief Joseph & the Flight of the Nez Perce: The Untold Story of an American Tragedy by Kent Nerburn
That All People May be One People, Send Rain to Wash the Face of the Earth by Chief Joseph

NELSON MANDELA

A Long Walk to Freedom by Nelson Mandela

ARCHBISHOP DESMOND TUTU

The Rainbow People of God: The Making of a Peaceful Revolution by Desmond Tutu
Believe: The Words and Inspiration of Archbishop Desmond Tutu by Desmond Tutu

Dr. MARSHALL ROSENBERG

Nonviolent Communication: A Language of Life by Dr Marshall Rosenberg

DANILO DOLCI

Fire Under the Ashes: The Life of Danilo Dolci by James McNeish
The World is One Creature by Danilo Dolci

MAIREAD CORRIGAN & BETTY WILLIAMS

Mairead Corrigan McGuire & Betty Williams: Making Peace in Northern Ireland by Sarah Buscher & Bettina Ling
Mairead Corrigan, Betty Williams: Two Women Who Ignored Danger in Campaigning for Peace in Northern Ireland by Richard Deusch

PETER BENENSON

Peter Benenson: Taking a Stand Against Injustice Amnesty International by David Winner
Diplomacy of Conscience: Amnesty International and Changing Human Rights Norms by Ann Marie Clark

TARIQ KHAMISA

Azim's Bardo: A Father's Journey from Murder to Forgiveness by Azim Khamisa

The Secrets of the Bulletproof Spirit: How to Bounce Back from Life's Hardest Hits by Azim Khamisa & Jillian Quinn

DR. ALBERT SCHWEITZER

For All that Lives, the Words of Albert Schweitzer by Ann Atwood and Erica Anderson.

Out of My Life and Thought: An Autobiography by Albert Schweitzer

THE MOTHERS OF THE PLAZA DE MAYO

Circle of Love over Death: The Story of the Mothers of the Plaza de Mayo by Matilde Mellibovsky

Revolutionizing Motherhood: The Mothers of the Plaza de Mayo by Marguerite Guzman Bouvard

MEENA

Meena, Heroine of Afghanistan: The Martyr Who Founded RAWA, the Revolutionary Association of the Women of Afghanistan by Melody Ermachild Chavis

Zoya's Story: An Afghan Woman's Struggle for Freedom by Zoya

With All Our Strength: The Revolutionary Association of the Women of Afghanistan by Anne E. Brodsky

THE DALAI LAMA

Freedom in Exile: The Autobiography of the Dalai Lama by Dalai Lama

JOHN MUIR

The Story of My Boyhood and Youth by John Muir

Meditations of John Muir: Nature's Temple compiled by Chris Highland

ALBERT EINSTEIN

Einstein in America: The Scientist's Conscience in the Age of Hitler and Hiroshima by Jamie Sayen

FATHER GREGORY BOYLE

Tattoos on the Heart: The Power of Boundless Compassion by Father Gregory Boyle

Dr. CATHERINE HAMLIN

The Hospital by the River: A Story of Hope by Catherine Hamlin

Catherine's Gift: Stories of Hope from the Hospital by the River by John Little

OTHER RESOURCES

Hidden Treasure: Uncovering the Truth in Your Life Story by Gangaji

Peacemakers: Winners of the Nobel Prize by Ann T. Keen

Social Change 2.0: A Blueprint for Reinventing Our World by David Gershon

Chelsea McGraw: www.chelseamcgraw.com

There is a free nonviolent course by Colman Mc Carthy at salsa.net/peace/conv/. Much good information here. American University in Washington, DC also has courses and training in Peace Studies.

The Ashoka Foundation, *How to Change the World.* ashoka.org/leadempathy

Fellowship of Reconciliation—working for peace, justice, and nonviolence since 1915. forusa.org

I found out about *World Pulse Magazine / Global Issues Through the Eyes of Women* from my dear friend Louise Pare, Ph.D. I see it as a valuable way to support and connect women with other women around the world. You will learn of many organizations working to help women in need, and have the opportunity to make important global connections. Their website is www.worldpulse.com.

27131670R00031

Made in the USA
Charleston, SC
01 March 2014